VIC

Victor & Barry's

KELVINSIDE COMPENDIUM

A Meander Down Memory Close

Published by 404 Ink
www.404Ink.com
@404Ink

First published in Great Britain, 2024

Project management: Laura Jones-Rivera
Editing: Brian Donaldson
Proofreading: Heather McDaid
Cover and interior design: Luke Bird
Co-founders and publishers of 404 Ink:
Heather McDaid & Laura Jones-Rivera

Print ISBN: 978-1-912489-93-0
Ebook ISBN: 978-1-912489-94-7

Printed and bound in Great Britain by Bell and Bain Ltd, Glasgow.

Acknowledgements from Alan and Forbes: Thanks to Jane Barrie, Ray Diggins, Derek Easton, Kathryn Howden, Peter Ling and Mary Darling for photos and memorabilia. Thanks to Grant Shaffer for the illustrations of Victor and Barry in the endpapers. Thanks to Jack Hopkins for original music notation and Gordon Dougall for the arrangement of the new song. Thanks to Vivienne Clore.

All photos from Alan Cumming and Forbes Masson's personal archives except where otherwise stated. Every effort has been made to obtain the necessary permissions with reference to illustrative copyrighted material. We apologise for any omissions in this respect and will be pleased to make the appropriate acknowledgements in any future edition. Main cover photo by David Morrissey. All photos from STV productions provided with permission. Photo of Nicola Sturgeon by Scottish Government, 2020 (edits made). Photos of Forbes as Emcee by Derek Easton. Photo of Michael Boyd by Ellie Kurttz. Photo of Bob Clyde by Richard Gurney. Photo of Getting Past It production and other performances by Alan Wylie. Photo of Alan Cumming and Forbes Masson on the cover of The List in 1987 by David Williams. Photo of Forbes in Doctor Faustus by Sean Hudson courtesy of Tron Theatre. Official portrait of David Steel by UK Parliament: https://members.parliament.uk/member/949/portrait (edits made). Photo of David Jackson Young by Florence Dégeilh. Photo of David Morrissey by Simon Annand. In the Scud photos by David Morrissey. Photo of Nicholas Parsons by Featureflash Photo Agency / Shutterstock.com. Photos of Alan Cumming and Forbes Masson from 2022 by Tommy Ga-Ken Wan. All paper textures, affixings and frames © Adobe Stock.

Victor & Barry's

KELVINSIDE COMPENDIUM

A Meander Down Memory Close

ALAN CUMMING
& FORBES MASSON

published by

Hello & Welcome

Hello and welcome, we're glad you've came to see us
Let's leave behind what's serious and have a real good laugh
Ha! Ha!
Hello and welcome, sit back in relaxation
We'll make light of the situation
Ye huv tae laugh or you'd weep

This is the sad bit cos we've got to have it
To make sure our show isn't samey
But don't worry, the sad bits won't tarry
Thanks to Barry McLeish and Victor MacIlvaney
We're terribly talented, oh it's a curse!
We're a couple of upfront go-getters
We were born in the west which proves we are the best
Cos youse'll know Glasgow smiles better

Our show is well done, it took some concentration
To write the songs and funny bits and all the synco-pation
Hello and welcome, please don't get too ecstatic
As we unfold dramatically
The Victor and Barry show

Our business is show business
and we want to do a deal with…

Youse!

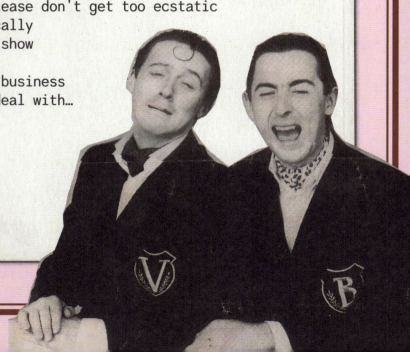

Foreword

by Nicola Sturgeon, MSP

In 1982, Alan Cumming and Forbes Masson met at the Royal Scottish Academy of Music and Drama in Glasgow, now the Royal Conservatoire of Scotland. The Kelvinside Men were born, and the rest, as they say, is history. Victor and Barry (a homegrown parody of the luvvies of Glasgow's leafy West End) really has stood the test of time, and it's hard to believe that this beloved double act is now over 40 years young.

It feels like no time at all since the youthful Victor MacIlvaney and Barry McLeish first bounced onto the theatrical boards of Scotland's stages, bringing a chic style that only the Kelvinside Young People's Amateur Dramatics Arts Society (or KYPADAS for short) could. In 1984, Victor and Barry donned their trademark monogrammed blazers and headed to the Edinburgh Fringe. As performers through the ages have done, our duo handed out flyers on the Royal Mile.

Two years later, they released a cassette (yes, cassette!) album called *Are We Too Loud?*, and in 1989 they opened at the Sydney Opera House. And just five short years on, Victor and Barry performed at The London Palladium, as part of a Lyric Hammersmith theatre fundraiser, where they said a final goodbye to audiences. Or so we thought…

Back then, in a typically Scottish manner, this comedic couple downplayed themselves as 'just two guys who try to do our best, we're so surprised at our success'. They clearly never imagined the legacy that would be created. Perhaps prophetically, Alan and Forbes have truly gone on to live *The High Life*. Their achievements are remarkable and vast, from the Royal Shakespeare Company to blockbuster movies and Emmy-winning TV. Now, of course, we might say that none of this could have happened without Victor and Barry.

It's brilliant to see the 'trendy thespians' returning to our lives, when we need a laugh most of all. I am certain that Victor and Barry's welcome encore will have us laughing and smiling as much as we did all those years ago.

INTRODUCTION

Incredibly, it has now been forty years since Victor MacIlvaney and Barry McLeish, collectively known by the showbiz moniker *Victor and Barry* first appeared, blinking and mewling like some theatre-obsessed kittens who, unbeknownst to them, were about to be flung oh so soon into the hurly burly whirlpool of international fame and glory. Forty years since they dragged their alma mater, the Kelvinside Young People's Amateur Dramatic Arts Society, out from the dingy shadows of community theatre obscurity and vomited them onto the global stage. Forty years of genteel double entendres and harmonious odes to the pleasures of yesteryear and what might have been. Forty years of making the surreal real. Forty years of putting the A in show business.

Victor and Barry are the epitome of the expression 'big in the '80s'. Annoyingly, they were also a little big in the first bit of the '90s too, so that phrase doesn't really pan out very satisfactorily; much like Victor and Barry themselves, in fact, who completely disappeared from the face of the Scottish showbiz scene in 1994 and were rumoured to have actually died on stage. As in died and no longer breathing, not died as in went down very badly with an audience which, of course, had happened to them many times.

But apparently rumours of their deaths have been greatly exaggerated, and the two can still be spotted strolling the leafy suburban lanes near the home they have shared for many decades at 22B Lacrosse Terrace, Kelvinside, Glasgow G12.

Although they now shun the limelight and *have* been referred to in the Scottish tabloid press as the Gay Garbos, they agreed to grant a rare interview for this book. It is, after all, a celebration of the incredible five decades since they made their first ever professional appearance at Hallibees Café Cabaret in Glasgow's glorious West End.

22B Lacrosse Terrace is not the gaudy McMansion you might expect two Scottish entertainment luminaries to reside in, but a modest bijou maisonette in an unassuming Kelvinside side street, handy for both the Kelvinbridge underground station and the WRI Hall. The latter is home to the Kelvinside Young People's Amateur Dramatic Arts Society (KYPADAS for short), the foremost amateur musical company in the whole of Scotland, if not Glasgow.

The pair appear at their front door in trademark monogrammed silk dressing gowns, and aside from a few tell-tale signs of the passing years since their mysterious departure from our stages, screens and hearts (Victor's gown is a little more figure hugging than it once was, Barry's slicked back raven locks could do with a touch up at the roots), they haven't changed a bit. Actually, that is not true. They are both a bit wrinkly.

Posters of some of their greatest musical triumphs at KYPADAS adorn the walls of their lounge – *Victor and His Amazing Multi-Textured Cardigan*, *West End Story*, *The Sound of Mucus* – and the top of their baby grand is festooned with photographs of them in their glory days. That's them smiling ferociously next to the many legends they have worked with, both local homegrown talents they nurtured to stardom like Sheena Easton, as well as international stars such as Anne Diamond and Sooty.

After the initial welcome and small talk, and once the tea has been poured and the scones have been dispensed, they say they are ready to address the elephant in the room.

'Hello Nelly!' says Victor.

'What's your address?' adds Barry. It is some time before conversation resumes as Victor and Barry laugh long and loudly at their quips, and repeatedly compliment each other on their enduring comedy timing.

Once they have regained their composure, they agree it is indeed time to come clean and finally pull back the curtain to reveal the true story behind this modern Caledonian myth. It has been decades, after all, since they have allowed access like this. Surely the moment had arrived to confess everything.

'Hold on to your chapeaux,' Victor purred cryptically.

'Because this story is a beezer!'

'It's a stoatir, so it is!' chimed in Barry.

The pair then began to journey through the mists of time to their last public performance on Sunday, the 20th of February, 1994, at none other than a little venue known as the London Palladium.

Barry solemnly placed his cup and saucer down on the folding table between us and began.

'The received norman wisdom is that after reaching the pinnacle of theatrical glory, having performed on those boards trodden by so many of the showbiz greats…'

'…The Krankies, Rod Hull and Emu, Princess Margaret,' Victor added helpfully.

'…that we had decided to hang up our cravates, turn our blazered backs on all the fame and the adulation,' Barry continued.

Just then Victor slammed his fist down on the arm of his lazy boy recliner for dramatic effect, forgetting he was holding a raisin scone in his hand. The crumbs went everywhere but he was undeterred.

'Nothing could be farther from the truth!'

It turns out that the real story behind the pair's evaporation from the amateur musical firmament is more shocking, more full of surprising twists and even less believable than the juiciest *River City* plotline.

After their Palladium triumph they boarded an overnight Stagecoach bus home to Glasgow, then took a fast black directly to their preferred culinary retail emporium – Presto's on Byres Road – 'to replenish our pantry with some tasty and revivifying morsels.'

Victor takes up the story: 'Just as we were debating the nutritional benefits of a bumper pack of Mr Kipling Cherry Bakewells, we spotted two uncouth youths skulking by the satsumas.'

The two young men in question were Callum Skink and Mungo Byrne, co-creators of The Dennistoun Drama Collective, a recent arrival on Glasgow's amdram scene and the complete antithesis of everything Victor and Barry stood for at the Kelvinside Young People's Amateur Dramatic Arts Society.

Callum Skink and Mungo Byrne were working class, idealistic and worshipped at the altar of a man Victor and Barry refer to through gritted teeth as 'that little Teutonic killjoy'. The rest of us know him as Bertolt Brecht. Callum Skink and Mungo Byrne believed the musical form was finished and worse – that Victor and Barry were cultural traitors for daring to perform south of Berwick on Tweed!

'Now, don't get us wrong,' explains Barry. 'Victor and I are no strangers to experimental theatre. Our radical production of *The Kirkintilloch Chalk Circle* took the theory of alienation to new depths!'

'Oh yes indeed. You have never seen an audience more alienated!' added Victor. 'We are all for the oppression of the proletariat being confronted in light operatic form but we felt that things had gone too far with Callum and Mungo's recent picketing of the WRI Hall on each of the three nights of our sell-out run of *Call Me Madam*.'

'Madam!' responded Barry, and once more the tale was interrupted for several minutes while the pair tried to regain their composure after guffawing at their own joke.

'Oh dearie me!' they eventually crowed together for what would not be the first time in our long discussion, the sign that they were now able to move on.

Unwilling to engage in a dialectic about the merits of Goethe versus Meredith Wilson so early in the morning after a mostly sleepless night on the bus, Victor and Barry diverted their trajectory towards the freezer section of Presto's. But when they saw Callum Skink and Mungo Byrne appear round the corner by the Birds Eye frozen meals, they swiftly pretended to be engrossed in a party platter of Presto's pink Pacific prawns.

A little too swiftly apparently, for they both tripped on the lip of the walk-in freezer door!
    'We were plunged face first into an icy pile of Oceania's finest!' explained Barry.

However, once inside the freezer they realised they had shaken off their adversaries or 'those two little theatrical Trotskyites' as Victor referred to them, and determined to wait it out until the coast was completely clear then recommence their retail roundelay.

'Alas, it was not to be', said Victor, picking up the narrative reins, clearly still disturbed by the memory. 'As the receding laughter of Callum Skink and Mungo Byrne crystallised before our very eyes we discovered the door to the freezer was jammed! We later learned that the cause was a crushed can of Tennent's Special Brew, shoved through the door handles, effectively imprisoning us in that ice palace!'

Having no other choice, Kelvinside's favourite sons hunkered down and waited to be rescued by a friendly shelf stacker. But alas, that was never to be! Unbeknownst to Victor and Barry, that very day Presto's was closing and being turned into a Safeway.
    'And how utterly ironic was that?' whispered Victor dramatically. 'As in no way did it turn out to be safe for us!'
    'Very clever, Victor!' complimented Barry as he reached for the teapot and offered us all a top up.
    'Thanks, Barry,' Victor replied, proffering his cup and saucer.

After the sugar and milk had been added, ('Oat for Victor, cow gives him the bloat!'), Barry continued the harrowing tale.

'Unbeknownst to us, as we curled up for a much needed and nippy nap - using a bag of Wild Alaskan Halibut portions as a pillow, incidentally - the freezer that we thought was a mere temporary penitentiary was that very evening, as part of the whole Presto/Safeway transmogrification, being taken to be disposed of in a landfill!'

'And even worse,' added Victor, shuddering, 'a landfill in an area of Glasgow so scabby, so barren, so post-apocalyptic that nary a burgher of our dear green place would ever set foot there.

That area was Finnieston. But the Finnieston of today - widely considered as Glasgow's hipster central - is a far cry from the Finnieston of thirty years ago.

'In 1992, we didn't even know the word artisanal,' says Barry, though he pronounced it art is anal.
    'And in Finnieston,' Victor deadpanned, 'let me tell assure you, there was neither!'

And so incredibly, Victor and Barry were trapped underground inside an industrial freezer unit for three decades, and they would be there to this day were it not for a change in Glasgow City Council's archeological guidelines for new buildings.
    'Construction people have to fully dig up and examine the soil on all new building sites nowadays,' explains Barry. 'Or the council won't consent to any new erections.'

Amazingly, Victor and Barry manage to find joy in not just their own miraculous escape but also place it in the wider context of ensuring cultural landmarks are never unknowingly decimated in the future.

'Apparently people had been erecting concrete monstrosities on top of the homes of important historical Scottish figures like Robert the Bruce and Arthur Montford,' says Victor, clearly horrified.
    'Of course, they weren't actually still buried in the landfill like we were,' Barry adds. 'But the law that precipitated our emancipation from prawn purgatory also ensures the legacy of other showbiz legends.'

But how did these legends manage to stay alive, underground and semi-frozen, for so long?
    'We know it sounds like a fishy tale!' begins Barry.
    'That's very funny, Barry!' says Victor supportively.
    'Do you think so, Victor?'
    'No, not really.'

But seriously, how did they do it? The pair described how they survived by each day blowing on items from the vast cache of frozen food to heat them up, as well as engaging in a rigorous programme of exercise, doing pull ups on the freezer's meat hooks. The combination of sheer protein and muscle building seems to have been the key to their survival according to nutritional experts and doctors who examined them upon their release.

They also kept their minds active by writing new musical shows inspired by the chilly circumstances they found themselves in.

'*Seven Bridies for Seven Brothers*, for example,' lists Victor.

'*Little Shop of Hot Dogs*,' continues Barry. 'And my particular fave, *The King Prawn Ring and I*.'

But their ingenious methods of creating these shows in such exceptional conditions is even more inspiring.

'We achieved these great artistic achievements,' begins Barry modestly, 'by fashioning a pianoforte of frozen fish fingers that banged against a range of polystyrene tubs of Thousand Island dressing. Each individual tub of the tangy fluid was drained to create ambient passages that recreated the chromatic scale, all thanks to Victor's perfect pitch.' Victor smiled at the memory.
  'Thank you, Barry. We used frozen string fries to create the higher octaves, and we even fashioned a set of bagpipes out of bits of octopus!'

When Victor and Barry's ages come up – a topic they have always guarded fiercely – they were delighted to explain a very pleasing by-product of their icy ordeal.
  'We have been literally frozen in time and so have not aged a single day since 1994!' Victor laughed. 'Our skin is as plump and full as it was then, thanks also to our entirely protein diet and the left over Thousand Island dressing, which we used as a moisturiser.'
  Barry adds that they both find it immensely gratifying to have been so inadvertently ahead of the skin care curve and to discover on their release back into non-seafood society that everyone today freezes their faces!
  'And nobody has slurped down more fish oil than us!' adds Victor. 'The amount of gallons of omega oil that slid down our gullets is monumental.'

Of course, after such a long albeit inadvertent exile, it must have been startling to discover so many changes to their beloved Kelvinside, to Glasgow itself and indeed Scotland. Surprisingly one of the most shocking changes to them is that

the supermarket on Byres Road where their ordeal began – formerly Presto's, then a Safeway – is now a Waitrose.

'I just never thought I'd see the day we would have Waitrose in Scotland', says Victor, a little tearful. 'It's a consumer miracle.'

The pair note that while there have indeed been many changes in the political and cultural landscape in their absence – a new Scottish parliament and the axing of Scottish Television's *Take The High Road* being two of the most revolutionary that spring immediately to their minds – it is heartening to also note that some things have not changed at all and have stayed, like Victor and Barry, frozen in time for the past three decades.
  'Kirsty Wark, for instance'.
  'And the Scottish theatre critics!'

When I remind them that this book, this scrapbook of memories and reminiscences, was actually the idea of Forbes Masson and Alan Cumming, their faces light up.
  'Oh, we love them,' says Barry. 'The ginger one is very funny.'
  'Alan and Forbes are two of our biggest superfans and I believe still dabble as part time professional thespians,' Victor continues.

They go on to reveal that it is not just the thirty year anniversary of Victor and Barry's extraordinary disappearance that is being memorialised via this tome. It is also, inconceivably, forty years since Victor and Barry first performed at the Edinburgh Fringe Festival, and forty two years since they first met Forbes and Alan. 'They were two pesky young drama students at the Academy, and they came round to the flat, desperate for our theatrical wit and wisdom', explains Barry. And what advice did the amdram veterans give to those fresh faced loons?

'Oh well,' Victor begins, 'the advice we gave them then is the advice we'd give them today: Never turn your back on the audience!'

'Be as big as you like as long as you mean it!' adds Barry.

'And never buy teeth from a catalogue', they conclude together.

1982

THE BIRTH OF VICTOR AND BARRY

Alan

It may be 40 years since we first performed Victor and Barry at the Edinburgh Fringe, but as this book is published in 2024, it's actually 42 years since we first created them. Yes, that's right! 42!

It was December 1982, the end of our first term at the Royal Scottish Academy of Music and Drama (now the Royal Conservatoire of Scotland) in Glasgow. College tradition dictated that first-year drama students perform a cabaret for the rest of the school on a Friday night just before the Christmas break. For both of us, getting into the Academy was a form of escape from lives and careers our parents wanted

for us, and this cabaret would be our debut performance in front of not just our first-year peers, but the older, sophisticated second and third years. It was a big deal.

Forbes

The day before my audition for drama school, the BBC aired the first episode of *Kids from Fame* and I thought drama school was going to be just like that, with people dancing in leotards on tables and cars, and singing sentimental songs. It turned out to be rather more sober, though I do remember much hilarity on the first day when I went to buy a dance belt with some of my fellow students. The camp shopkeeper eyed us young pups up and down, pointed at my colleagues individually and said, respectively, 'large, medium' and then when he got to me, said with a wry smile, 'extra small'.

But we actually DID wear leg warmers and terry towelling headbands in movement class. Those early days at drama school were so exciting. I felt I had found my home, the complete antithesis of what I encountered at secondary school where I had been bullied for being speccy, sensitive and ginger.

Alan

Between leaving high school and arriving at the Academy at the ripe old age of 17, I spent a year working at DC Thomson in Dundee where, amongst other things, I interviewed pop stars like Toyah Willcox and Bucks Fizz, and also wrote the horoscopes for the *Dundee Evening Telegraph*! But my real passion was the Carnoustie Theatre Club, where for a few years I had been acting in various plays and pantos, and then one musical, *My Fair Lady*, with the Carnoustie Musical Society. The latter was remarkable for the fact that I was originally cast as Freddy Eynsford-Hill, Eliza Doolittle's youthful suitor, but when the elderly gent playing Colonel Pickering fell ill just a few weeks before the four-night run began, guess who was asked to step in and replace him? Yes, 17-year-old me! And this wasn't a youth group! There were many age-appropriate male company members who could have stepped into the old colonel's musical shoes. But instead, I appeared, a sea of talcum powder in my hair and a mass of wrinkles drawn on my face, and saved the day! I think, more than 40 years later, Colonel Pickering is still the oldest person I have ever played!

While I was a pretty late convert to the amdram world, Forbes had caught the bug at a much earlier age…

Forbes

'You started singing in the pram,' my mother always said to me. Even as a baby, I used to sing along when she took me to rehearsals of her amateur musical group. My mother, Lilias Masson Robertson, and her sister-in-law, J Helen M. Robertson M.B.E., were founder members of the Falkirk and District Bohemian Amateur Operatic and Dramatic Society. Founded in 1948, it was the foremost amateur musical company in the whole of Scotland, if not Falkirk…

My aunt Helen was rehearsal pianist as well as president of the company, and my mum was Honorary Vice President but also danced and performed. In 1968, she played a memorable Mrs Pearce in the Scottish amateur premiere of, coincidentally, *My Fair Lady*. They also had a massive hit with *The Sound of Music*.

My mum was quite shy, and as she got older she stopped performing and became the prompter. As a toddler I would sit beside her in the darkened wings of Falkirk Town Hall as she whispered, loudly and often, when onstage performers forgot their lines. When I was eight, I played one of Fagin's boys in the Scottish amateur premiere of *Oliver!* and I got to sing. Not just from a pram. The Bohemians had a very high standard of production and their shows were always sold out; many of the performers 'could have gone professional' as audience members would say. One of them did. David Marshall, who had been an amazing Fagin in *Oliver!* and Captain Von Trapp in *The Sound of Music*, chucked in his job at the bank and went to drama school. He later became David Gant, achieving fame playing opposite Julie Andrews in the film *Victor/Victoria*.

I had been completely bitten by the bug and wanted to follow in David's footsteps so I joined the Falkirk Children's Theatre. In *The Wizard of Oz*, I played a soldier in the Ozian army and the munchkin coroner (my dad, Norman, sold gravestones so there was always an air of death about me!).

I played Pinocchio in another show and my fake nose fell off mid song!

Alan

I also did a few plays at Carnoustie High School, one of which was the trial scene from *The Merchant of Venice*. The one with all the nuns was called *Bonaventure*. My big break, though, was playing Bunthorne in the school's production of Gilbert and Sullivan's *Patience*. When my big brother Tom saw me as the aesthetic poet, swanning around onstage holding aloft a lily, his only comment was, 'You're just like that at home!'

Forbes

My aunt organised a concert party of amateur performers who went round old folks' homes. At the age

of 11 I became part of this troupe, covering hits like Jimmy Osmond's 'Long Haired Lover from Liverpool' to the elderly and infirm who had no viable means of escape. My mum was also part of the show and would read Scottish comic short stories aloud.

All the local performers would gather in aunt Helen's kitchen where tea was always stewing on her old coal Aga. I sat agog listening to the local amateur-musical and drama gossip. She had cupboards and cupboards full of sheet music ranging from old music-hall songs up to the latest 1970s hits. One of those pieces of sheet music inspired one of Victor and Barry's first songs, 'We'll Gather Lilacs' by Ivor Novello.

When I was older, I sold programmes and ice creams at the Bohemians performances, sneaking backstage to watch from the wings. My mum had a gift for comic writing and would come up with parody lyrics to songs from that year's production, with funny mentions of the cast or things that had happened during the run. These were handed out at the last night of the show. So, I guess a penchant for parody was clearly in my gingery genes. Every Saturday I'd be down the local library where I would wander around browsing their collection of comedy books and records. Billy Connolly, The Goons, Round the Horne, Julian and Sandy, Monty Python, Peter Sellers: I would read and play their stuff at home and really laugh.

KEITH FRASER, DAVID ROBERTSON, BARRY JENKINS, CALUM BENNIE,
SHELDON MILLARD, ROY WILSON, GRAHAM ROBERTSON, COLIN CADGER, STUART STAMPER,
IAN BAILEY, BARRIE CLIFFORD, ALISTAIR FINLAY,
RODNEY SMITH, ALISTAIR McMILLAN, DAVID WRIGHT,
JOHN FERGUSON, PAUL HUNTER, KEVIN McINTOSH, DEREK NELSON,
FORBES ROBERTSON, EWING STRACHAN, STUART FORBES

Alan

I loved those few years of doing plays and musicals with the Carnoustie amateur companies. My home life was pretty difficult, so the chance to escape and immerse myself deep into different characters far removed from my own existence was a much-needed balm. My best friend (also called Alan) had a girlfriend who'd been a member of the theatre club and left to study drama at a college in Glasgow. This was a revelation to me: you could actually go to college and study this stuff? And wait, what? You could actually maybe become an actor and that would be your job?! Gamechanger!

Forbes

I joined the Falkirk Players, where I met two directors, Russell Boyce and Ronnie Mackie, who worked at the RSAMD. They suggested I audition for the school of

drama. When I broached the subject with my parents, my mum was all for it, but my dad said, 'No son of mine is going to drama school in Glasgow.' He wanted me to become an accountant.

Heeding my father's advice and with my tail between my legs, I left school to study accountancy and business studies at Clackmannan College (which later merged with Falkirk College to become Forth Valley College), with a view to following in my father's footsteps in the family business. I hated it and spent more and more time in amateur shows, so much so that I used to fall asleep in class. In 1981 I was in the Falkirk Bohemians' Scottish amateur premiere of *Joseph and His Amazing Technicolor Dreamcoat*. That's me on the left below in the mini toga.

The guy playing Joseph was called Ray Diggins, who was something of a star in the local amdram scene; when I made my debut in *Oliver!*, he had played the Artful Dodger. He spoke to me about trying to get the rights for *Cabaret* and asked if I wanted to play the Emcee. We formed a new company and put it on ourselves. I relished the chance to play the Emcee, and during rehearsals I was asked to go and pick up the gorilla costume used in the 'If You Could See Her' number. So, in early 1982, I took the train through to Glasgow and then the underground to Kelvinbridge to the costume shop. That was the first time I had ever been to Glasgow's West End. I decided to give it a go and applied to audition for the RSAMD.

Alan

Many years later, the Emcee in *Cabaret* would be a very important character in my life too! I played him in Sam Mendes' production at London's Donmar Warehouse in 1993/4 and won a Tony for playing him on Broadway in 1998. And I did it again on Broadway in 2014! I can't quit you, *Cabaret*!

Forbes

At the time, RSAMD had only two drama courses. One was purely for acting, the other was a degree course involving acting, directing, creativity and teaching. I just wanted to do the acting course, but as a compromise to appease my fretful father, I decided to go for the degree. 'Something to fall back on,' he said. In hindsight, he was right. Doing that course helped me be very proactive and creative in my career. Lots of my colleagues in the amdram world were so supportive of my upcoming audition. Ronnie Mackie helped me choose pieces and coached me and I performed them to my pals who gave me the thumbs-up. I auditioned and, after a few weeks of nail biting, found out I had been accepted.

SOUND OF SUCCESS AS SHOW IS SOLD OUT

By ARTHUR JAMES

WHEN THE CURTAIN goes up tonight for the open-ing of Falkirk Amateur Operatic Society's "The Sound of Music" at Callendar Park Falk...

Now rec...

Members of the new local drama group, Theatre Forward.

STEP FORWARD WITH NEW THEATRE GROUP

For their inaugural production, the recently-formed "Theatre Forward" amateur musical society will present the hit show "Cabaret" as part of this year's Falkirk Festival.

Theatre Forward was formed in April of last year by a group of young adults whose objective was to produce modern musicals of a type which had never previously been available to Falkirk audiences and by so doing, to encourage the active involvement in theatre of other young adults, society president Ray Diggins said:

"For a new society to present a full scale musical show is an exciting but major undertaking. However, Cabaret is a terrific show and everyone is working so tremendously hard that we have already achieved our initial objectives. Also, the active support and encouragement of some of the other local clubs has been over-whelming and we are all looking forward to a really successful show."

Cabaret will be presented in Callendar Park College Theatre from Tuesday, March 9 to Saturday, March 13. Tickets are available from the Festival booking office at the Steeple or from society members.

FALKIRK BOHEMIAN AMATEUR OPERATIC AND DRAMATIC SOCIETY

SEASON 1970

PRESIDENT'S FOREWORD

LADIES AND GENTLEMEN,

On behalf of the Falkirk Bohemians it is my privilege and pleasure to welcome you to the Scottish Premiere of "THE SOUND OF MUSIC." The film, "The Sound of Music," enjoyed enormous success in Scotland and, as this is the first time the show has been produced in our "ain" country, I hope you will find equal pleasure in it.

We are fortunate in having Douglas Sneddon as Producer and Irene Langlands as Ballet Mistress, their work is well known and they are well-liked by the members of the Society. This year we have a new Musical Director—one Pat Deans—new as Musical Director but well-thought-of in the past as our Pianist. Unfortunately Pat (Mrs. Derek Deans), owing to a happy indisposition, is not on the conductor's rostrum and her place is being taken by that weel-kent Musical Director of Larbert Operatic Society, Peter Watson. We are deeply indebted to Peter Watson and we thank him very much indeed for his help. We also thank the President and members of Larbert Operatic Society for making this possible.

I feel very honoured indeed to write this note as President of this Society and take this opportun... of thanking the Committee and members for making my hobby such an enjoyable one. ...thank you... for your support in the past, for coming to our sho...

Alan

I'm so glad I did the BA course instead of just the pure acting one. It taught me many things but the biggest and most important was that acting should be a communal thing. It's not, and should not, just be all about you. We studied so many more facets of the theatre than just acting, and that not only helped us become writers, producers and directors as we got older, it also made us much better actors. The course taught us not to be insular, not to obsess about ourselves and our acting. I think Forbes and I both have a lightness as performers, and an understanding of the fine line between laughter and tears: the two masks of the theatre. That, I am certain, is something we gained through doing such an eclectic degree course, so we approach acting as though we're children playing and not adults over-analysing and complicating matters.

Forbes

In the September of 1982 we both arrived in Glasgow to begin our studies. Here, at the RSAMD, I could belong. Specs-free (thanks to my new contact lenses), my ginger hair grew long, floppy and proud, and I became a true New Romantic with baggy trousers, geometric shirts, tukka boots, second-hand black dinner jackets from Flip and a cravate. And a hat. I remember going into a pub dressed like that one night and some guys threw peanuts at me. Obviously, I wasn't at home everywhere.

Alan

And so, towards the end of our first term we both put our names down for the First Year Cabaret. We were taking part in several turns, including a parody of Bucks Fizz (the Eurovision darlings I had interviewed back in Dundee, subtly renamed Ducks Piss for the evening), singing in a group rendition of a song of mine, 'Where Did Tomorrow Go?', as well as the obligatory 'Time Warp'.

Forbes

But then a fellow student suggested we did something together. Although we were in the same year, we were in different classes so didn't know each other very well, but we recognised a mutual creative spark. Alan made me laugh so much and I was in awe of his confidence, something I felt lacking in. As I told *The Guardian* in 2021: 'The first time I saw Alan I thought, god that guy is really interesting. There's something special about him. We quickly realised we had an almost telepathic way of writing and performing together.' In the same interview, Alan said of me: 'He was quirky, talented and good on the piano. He was also a little older because he'd gone to college to study accounting before he switched to drama, and as a result seemed like more of a man of the world.'

Alan

At the time Forbes was 19, and I was 17! But to paraphrase John Byrne, we had *everything* to live for. At the eleventh hour, just a few days before the cabaret was due to take place, we walked into a college rehearsal room one night after class.

On a recent weekend home, I had performed a monologue as a fuddy-duddy Glaswegian man named Victor MacIlvaney for an event in Carnoustie, so we had one funny name (which ultimately was assigned to Forbes). Neither of us were Glasgow natives so there was much about the city, and especially the West End, that was new and funny to us. We both loved the idea of parodying amateur dramatics given that, to varying degrees, our backgrounds were steeped in it.

Forbes

We both agreed that the Kelvinside, anglicised, posh Scottish accent had a degree of pretentiousness that was ideal for our creations. Almost like Stanley Baxter's *Parliamo Glasgow* in reverse.

Victor and Barry were artistes who 'could have gone professional' but chose not to, from a district in Glasgow that had aspirations to be posher than it was: Scots who were embarrassed at being Scots. We thought it would be funny if these two amdrammers came to lecture the third years about dramatic art. And sing some parody songs. With a few bum notes.

Something magical happened. The Victor and Barry muse descended, and about five minutes of material

was swiftly written. It was very rough and ready but Victor and Barry and the Kelvinside Young People's Amateur Dramatic Art Society was born!

Little did we think they would breathe for ten years and be remembered more than four decades later!

Alan

On the night of the cabaret, we began with a version of 'Willkommen', the Emcee's opening number from *Cabaret*, in which Victor and Barry mangled all the foreign pronunciations and ended with 'Vic and Barr-ay' instead of 'Cabar-et'.

When I performed 'Willkommen' on Broadway, I actually used some of Victor and Barry's gags from when *they* sang the song! Like when the song goes, 'wie geht's, comment ça va, do you feel good?' Barry had added, 'yes, I bet you do.' I totally pinched that as well as several other Victor and Barry ad-lib gems! When that production was licensed, they used the actual Broadway script including all those little additions, so Victor and Barry's ad-libs are still being heard every time *Cabaret* is performed around the globe! Can you imagine?!

Forbes

We went down an absolute storm. Even then, it was obvious there was real chemistry between us, and that something truly special was afoot. We also just had fun together. We were both newbies to the city and parodying what we saw Glasgow becoming, or at least aspiring to become. This was the early '80s, remember, the dawning of wine-bar culture and gentrification; it was the antithesis of the shipyards and that Glasgow hard man, *No Mean City* image.

And we were parodying ourselves, too. We were first-year drama students who had to wear tights and leg warmers for movement classes. And we were loud and theatrical on Buchanan Street!

Alan

We left college for the Christmas break, excited about these new discoveries. Unto us Victor and Barry were born!

CAFÉ CABARET – TERRY TOWELLING KELVINSIDE QUICHE

Alan

Victor and Barry's debut professional appearance was on Saturday 14th May 1983 at Hallibees Café Cabaret in Glasgow's West End. As young drama students and wannabe actors, all we could think about was getting an Equity card. This was the early '80s, the height of Margaret Thatcher's crusade to crush the unions and, especially, the idea of a closed-shop. At the time, Equity, the acting union, was one of the last closed shops which meant you had to be a member of that union to get work as a professional actor. Equally, it meant that you couldn't get an Equity card and become a member of the union without first getting an offer of professional work!

Forbes

Each repertory theatre had two Equity cards to give out a year, for acting assistant stage manager posts, which meant you'd play small parts as well as helping the stage managers run the show. But two per theatre didn't add up to very many and competition was fierce as it was open to not just students of the RSAMD, but everyone and anyone. Many great acting graduates didn't get an Equity card and so just simply couldn't work; they eventually fell into other jobs to get by. We were all obsessed with the notion that our dreams of acting could be so easily and unfairly quashed by this almost lottery system.

But there was a loophole… If you went through the cabaret department at Equity and showed them contracts to prove you had been paid to perform professionally in a few cabaret venues, you could get an Equity card that way, and so enter into the union. Suddenly, Victor and Barry weren't just fun characters to play in a skit for college mates: they were our entrée into the profession!

Alan

Hallibees was on Ruthven Lane, just off Byres Road and round the corner from Athole Gardens, home to our drama school annexe. For our first year we took classes there in a converted townhouse, only going into the centre of town to mix with other students for classes on Fridays. Hallibees was a wholefood café that had live entertainment most nights. We'd pass by it every day on our way to the annexe and sometimes ate lunch there. Forbes and I charmed the lady who ran it into giving us a gig, and she let us do a Saturday night supporting the jazz duo of Graham Whitelaw and Dick Lee.

We got changed into our costumes in the kitchen. The smell of cheesy lentil bake was overwhelming but we soldiered on, nervous as hell because neither of us had ever been paid actual money for performing anything in our lives before. We wore terry towelling dressing gowns (blue for me and red for Forbes), with matching trousers and cravates. Our hair was greased back and held in place with copious amounts of gel. Forbes stuck a little kiss curl to his forehead. He also wore ballet pumps and one leg warmer, a nod to our college movement classes.

Forbes

When the time came, we entered from the kitchen, wound our way through the packed tables with little candles flickering on them and stepped up onto the tiny, raised platform of a stage. There was a piano and a red velvet curtain behind us. No mics. The applause stopped, I began to play, and we were off.

In what was perhaps a sign of their precocious future, somehow Victor and Barry got top billing in this hand-drawn poster!

The skit we had performed for our drama-school cabaret was about Victor and Barry coming to impart their theatrical wisdom to the students, but now we began to fill out their back stories and create an augmented, heightened, surreal world for them to inhabit. We began to parody the pretensions of the times we were living in (the sheer prevalence of quiche!) via these two self-appointed ambassadors for the new Glasgow. Specifically, we spoke of their beloved home district of Kelvinside which they described as 'a mecca for culture, a magnet for music, a mangle for the arts in general.'

Alan

It was a vibrant and exciting time to be Scottish. Margaret Thatcher's policies had driven a huge cultural wedge between us and the south, and engendered, presumably accidentally, a resurgence of national pride and a desire to speak literally and metaphorically in our own voices. This confluence encouraged us to write about what we knew and to shine a light on our own experience as young Scots; we weren't going to just pretend to be from somewhere else. The concept of alternative cabaret was just beginning and so were we! And we must have done OK, because a month later we were asked back to headline our own show. Victor and Barry were now part of our lives, part of our identities, part of our future!

Bookings
041 334 8560

Licensed
till 11.00pm

HALLIBEES
61 Ruthven Lane, Byres Rd Glasgow G12

CAFÉ — CABARET

THE VICTOR & BARRY SHOW

"The voice of Kelvinside!"

"Puts the 'A' in showbusiness" - West End Times.

"Who?" - The Times.

"Victor and Barry portray a brilliant theatrical bent" - Boys' Own.

"A musical extravaganza" - Glasgow Herald.

WED. 29TH JUNE
at 7.30 pm.

Tel. 041-334 8860

Ruthven Lane, Byres Rd, Glasgow

Vat no. 316220795

Saturday: Cabaret: 14th May: The Victor & Bar

Starters : Lentil Soup
Garlic Bread
Bean Paté with Rollor C

Main Dishes : Cauliflower & Black-E

Janice Forsyth Remembers...

I've been lucky to have had tons of different jobs over the years in the arts, radio, TV and journalism; so many wonderful experiences all over the world, meeting countless fascinating people, and interviewing many of them on TV, radio and podcasts. I'm not saying that to brag (honest!) but to explain that it's all been so full-on over the decades, there's much that I don't recall. Although that may be partly down to enjoying a G&T or ten as part of the job. It's a professional obligation, you understand…

However, I'll never forget the first time I clapped eyes and ears on Victor and Barry. I was one of the team organising Mayfest, a pioneering Glasgow festival of popular theatre and music that had its socialist roots in the annual May Day march and celebrations that took place in the city. I remember like it was yesterday, arriving at the city's great Mitchell Library and popping into the Moir Hall, a room that cast off its municipal dullness in the evening and transformed into the glittering, shimmering Mayfest Club! It became a real hot ticket, with festival performers from Chicago, Cuba, USA and Eastern Europe popping in to watch a mix of cabaret, music and comedy.

I was there in the afternoon to do some admin but was stopped in my tracks by the sight and sound of two very young guys (cute as get oot), the redhead and the dark-haired boy with long eyelashes, wearing dressing gowns and cravates, rehearsing their turn for that night's Mayfest Club. And they were fantastic! So young but so accomplished (the songs were ace) with Forbes on piano, and the pair of them belting out funny, clever lyrics, with lashings of double entendres and fab harmonies, all lampooning a particular Glasgow West End 'awfully cultured' type. I had never heard anything like them before, but I knew there and then that I was witnessing something very special indeed. The rest is history, and subsequently, like so many fans across the world, I saw them perform in huge venues. But, Victor and Barry, I'll never forget my first time. Thank you for the joy and laughter.

50p

PARODY LYRICS

★

In those early days we mostly sang parodies, well-known songs with a few lyrics changed here and there. So, 'Cry Me a River' became 'Cry Me the Kelvin', 'Summertime' became 'Kelvinside'…

★

KELVINSIDE

Am   E   Am   E   Am   E
Kelvinside, that's where the living is easy
        Dm   F   B   E
Fish are jumping and the Kelvin is high
Am E Am E Am E
Oh your Daddy's rich, and your Mummy's good looking
        C Am D Dm Am E
So hush little baby, don't you cry
        Am E Am E Am E Am E
One of those mornings, you're going to wake up singing
        Dm   F   B   E
Then you'll sopread your wings and move up to Milngavie
Am   E   Am   E   Am   E
But til that morning, there's nothing that can harm youse
        C Am   D Dm Am E Am E
With Victor and Barry standing by

Kelvinside

SOMEWHERE OVER THE KELVIN

F Dm7 Am F7 Bb Bb/C Cm D7
Somewhere over the Kelvinbridge you'll find

Gm7 Bbm F D7   G7 F
There's a land that you've heard of once in the Evening Times

F Dm7 Am F7 Bb Bb/C Cm D7
Someday you'll wish upon a star

Gm7 Bbm F D7 G7 F
And wake up where the landlords are quite choosey

F Dm7 Am F7 Bb Bb/C Cm D7
Where riots never happen and the garden

Gm7 Bbm F D7 G7 F
Refuse is collected on a Tuesday

F Dm7 Am F7 Bb Bb/C Cm D7
Someday you'll wake up

Gm7 Bbm F D7 G7 F
Where the shows are far superior

F Dm7 Am F7 Bb Bb/C Cm D7
Where there has never been a flop

Gm7 Bbm F D7 G7 F
Our actors are the very top that's our criteria

If Robbie Coltrane can get a job at the BBC, why oh why can't we?

'We'll Gather Lilacs' remained pretty much the same but we walked down a Kelvinside lane instead of an English one, and 'My Way' became 'The Kelvinside Way'…
We sometimes went totally nuts and did parody medleys! Here is one that ranged from Cabaret to Man of La Mancha by way of Piaf and The Sound of Music…

Money makes the world go around, the world go around, the world go around
Money makes the world go around, of that we both are sure on being poor
Money money money money etc
When you haven't any steak in the freezer and you feel like some chilli
And you plead with your butcher for some mince
When you haven't any tonic in the fridge, and you're clean out of lemons
And you've nothing to put into your gins
When you haven't any Vim for the bath, and the place is like a midden
And you'd kill for a bottle of Flash
When these sort of things occur in your life it soon becomes apparent
That you've got to get some cash

Cream teas and cravattes and body shop eye gel
Paisley pyjamas and songs that don't rhyme well
Souvenir teaspoons from Rothesay in spring, these are a few of my favourite things
Chinese kimonos and fibres that wash well,
Music for pleasure and pickwick and K-Tel
Campari, advocaat, malibu, these are some drinks that I like, me too

When the bird drops, when the cats scratch, when we're feeling sad
We simply remember our favourite things and then we don't feel so bad
Non, nous regrettons rien
This is our quest, to sing you some songs, no matter how flat, no matter how long
And the world will be better for this, that two men with an urge to amuse
Still sing though their voices are hoarse, to reach the unreachable note

1984

SPOOKY SLEEPOVERS – 'RAVE' REVIEWS
LOWER LARGO – GONG GLORY

"Edinburgh, Edinburgh, Edinburgh! It's so lovely to be here at this time of year, when a little piece of Scotland is forever England!"

Our first ever publicity shot!!

Forbes

In the summer holidays between our second and final years at RSAMD, Victor MacIlvaney and Barry McLeish made the odyssey eastwards to perform *The Victor and Barry Show* at the Edinburgh Festival Fringe for the first time. Alan and I came along too, but not just to perform: we also had front-of-house and stage management duties too. Each night after *The Victor and Barry Show* came down, we quickly changed to then man the box office as well as operating lights and sound for The Arran Sweaters, a Scottish heuchter cheuchter parody duo created and performed by Alasdair McCrone and Alan Vicary. It was an exhausting and elating few weeks, and our first taste of the Festival magic and madness that we would return to again and again over the years.

Alan

The Academy had taken over a venue, the Harry Younger Hall, just off the Royal Mile, for the Festival's three weeks. A variety of shows were mounted there by students old and new, and even some staff: our movement teacher Pete Lincoln presented his one-man show *Talk of the Devil*. While we were on box-office duty for that production, a couple of besuited and well-groomed gentlemen asked for details of the show. When asked if they wanted to actually buy tickets, they were repulsed, and retorted, 'Oh no! We are here because we travel the world monitoring the use of the sign of Beelzebub. We must beware!' When we assured them that we were not fans of the fallen angel, they departed; though not entirely convinced. However, a seed had been planted, and one night soon after the visit of those bedevilled detectives, we missed our last train to Glasgow and ended up spending a spooky sleepover on the floor of what we were now convinced was a haunted hall.

Forbes

In addition to performing Victor and Barry, we also appeared in other shows: I was in the play *Pin-Ups* by fellow student Chris Smith, and Alan was in a devised piece, *Off the Rails*.

Before we opened at the Fringe, I had managed to wangle us a warm-up gig at Falkirk Town Hall where we performed (in what appears to be the cloakroom!) for my former Falkirk Players cohorts. Maybe not surprisingly, they were a little bit sniffy at one of their golden sons returning to parody what was effectively their raison d'être: amateur dramatics.

Alan

However, it wasn't all negative. Jeanna Lee (now Connell), one of Forbes' friends, suggested we change one of the lyrics in our parody of the 'You're Just in Love' duet from *Call Me Madam*. From then on, we would sing 'a rub down with a *rubber* glove' instead of the as-written velvet one. I would also wear a yellow rubber glove at this moment in the song just to ram home the point! Later, a floral hat was added too.

Forbes

To prepare for the Festival, we had leaflets printed to advertise the show, and each day we handed them out to bemused tourists as we strolled up and down the Royal Mile in costume and character (or caricature) with all the other hundreds of optimistic (and loud) performers trying to hawk their wares and ensnare an audience.

Alan

Around 4am one morning, as we stumbled out of Bannerman's Bar (our post-show watering hole of choice), we experienced our first taste of the bitter realities of showbusiness upon seeing one of those leaflets lying in the gutter, a muddy boot print besmirching its pink cheeriness. Our publicity campaign also featured a series of photos taken in Forbes' mum and dad's house and garden in Falkirk by his friend Derek Easton. He used an instamatic camera (a sort of Kodak Polaroid) that belonged to Forbes' uncle.

Forbes

The Victor and Barry Show premiered on August 20th 1984 and a few days later we got our first rave review on Radio Forth.

Act One Productions Present —
In Association with The Kelvinside Young People's
Amateur Dramatic Arts Society

The Victor & Barry Show

A Pot - Pourri of Words & Music
Brought to you
straight from the Heart
of Glasgow's
KELVINSIDE!

...GUST 20th to SEPTEMBER 1st (exc. S...

At 10.30 p.m.

At the HAR... YOUNGER HALL

...Box Office

...Champs E...
...(miss)
...End Time...
...) Leadi...
...Renee"

THE VICTOR AND BARRY SHOW

The truth is out!

The funniest show on the Fringe is at the Harry Younger Hall. The very camp Victor and Barry (accomplished actors Forbes Robertson and Alan Cumming) take us on a 45 minute pot-pourri of reminicences of their theatrical and musical triumphs with the Kelvinside Young People's Amateur Dramatic Art Society.

Go and see it- it's wonderful.

Bruce Henderson,
RADIO FORTH.

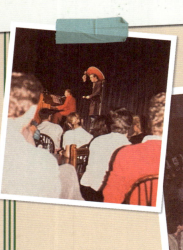

THE VICTOR AND BARRY SHOW
Act One Productions

THIS UNDEMANDING late evening entertainment from two young Scots will be particularly enjoyed by anyone from the crust-upper suburbs of Glasgow. Two camp, be-dressing-gowned musical actors recall their careers with Kelvinside Young People's Amateur Dramatic Art Society through a melange of songs.

The songs are, by and large, parodies of musical hits and are joined together with banter in a Kelvinside whine. This satire is very light indeed and the vocal abilities of the duo are, shall we say, limited; but they carry off a brief show with self-deprecating humour and panache. Some of the audience found the whole thing hilarious, others were simply bemused.

Andrew Marr

But we waited with bated breath for the review from *The Scotsman*, the one that really mattered. To be reviewed at all in *The Scotsman* during the Festival was a much-vaunted achievement then, and the content of that review could utterly dictate a show's success or failure. With literally thousands of shows to choose from, Fringe audiences used that paper and its extensive Festival coverage as a touchstone to whittle down the options and decide what to see. Each morning we would scurry to the newsagent and scour the columns to see if we had made it in. Finally, that day came. *The Victor and Barry Show* had a *Scotsman* review…

Alan

Not exactly a rave, no. Andrew Marr (yes, *that* Andrew Marr) was then a junior business correspondent at *The Scotsman*, presumably moonlighting as theatre critic during the all-hands-on-deck Festival month. Yes, Andrew Marr, who would later go on to become editor of *The Independent*, host of Radio 4's *Start the Week* and the eponymous *Andrew Marr Show*.

Andrew Marr gave Victor and Barry their first ever bad review. But they bit back!

Forbes

On the last night of the Festival, we were asked to perform at the Fringe Club; a huge honour as it was billed as *The Best of the Fest* show, a compendium of that year's finest Fringe acts. Still stinging from *The Scotsman* review, we decided to rewrite the Dean Friedman hit 'Lucky Stars' to express our feelings about it. The chorus went:

We can thank you, Andrew Marr
That you're not as smart as you'd like to think you are!

Playing to an audience of Festival-goers and young performers who understood the vagaries of a *Scotsman* review only too well, the song went down a storm. The final salvo was:

Those who can, act
Those who can't, write Fringe reviews for The Scotsman

Alan

The other abiding memory of that short run at the Harry Younger Hall was the evening we had no audience at all. It was the night of the annual fireworks display and we realised that doing a show which clashed with that Festival behemoth was going to make it tough to get a good crowd in. But surely we'd get someone: a few pyro-technophobes maybe? But no, not one single person. Only a solitary cat entered the theatre and slunk around unimpressed. We decided to do the show anyway. We could do with the practice, and if Victor and Barry had taught us anything, it was that the show must go on, audience or not.

Forbes

Our merch left a lot to be desired!

Alan

Later in 1984, when we returned for our final year of drama school, we put the show on again, a one-night only event in the Academy TV studio. We had both forgotten that this show had been filmed, and only recently it appeared on YouTube thanks to a fellow former RSAMD student, Charles Hamilton. This is the earliest recording of Victor and Barry performing together, and aside from the shock of us both lighting up cigarettes between songs, watching it again after so long was fascinating to see the nascent Victor and Barry characters and characteristics being developed.

Forbes

There were some forgotten gems: Victor mourning the death of his gerbils, Jean-Louis Barrault and Jean Genet; lines like, 'Kelvinside is to Glasgow what the Champs-Élysées is to Venice'; and, 'People come up to me and say, "Victor, your act is old-fashioned." Well, I just smile and say to them, "Yes it is. But isn't this crazy world we live in just a little bit old-fashioned too?"'

Alan

The whole show was dedicated as a protest against the Thatcher government's cuts that were beginning to hit the Academy's student grants. It also contains the first performance of what was to become a Victor and Barry mega-hit, 'Lower Largo Triangle', a pastiche of Barry Manilow's 'Bermuda Triangle'.

EMAS3 £1.00
ACT ONE PRODUCTIONS
VICTOR & BARRY SHOW
WED 22ND AUG/84

EMAS3 10
£1.00
ACT ONE PRODUCTIONS
VICTOR & BARRY SHOW
WED 22ND AUG/84
10.30PM

ACT ONE PRODUCTIONS
PRESENT
THE
VICTOR & BARRY SHOW
HARRY YOUNGER HALL
CANONGATE
WED 22ND AUG/84
10.30PM
£1.00
000023

Victor and Barry LIVE ON!

THE VICTOR AND BARRY SHOW
Hilarious reminiscences of the
People's Amateur Dramatic Art 9

Aug 20 – Sept 1 (not Sun) 10.3

We decide to get away and have some fun (fun! fun!)
Pack our bags and catch a bus for a weekend in the sun
I said Loch Lomond's too expensive
And I said Saltcoats isnae bad
I said I'd like to see Lower Largo
And I said Barry, are you mad?
Lower Largo triangle, it makes people disappear
Lower Largo Triangle, don't go too near!
Lower Largo, Lower Largo, sweeter than a spa-a-angle!

Forbes

The audience was made up of our college chums as well as a few industry types Ike Michael Boyd, who had recently taken over as artistic director of Glasgow's Tron Theatre. After seeing us at the Academy he asked us to take part in the Gong Show that he was starting in the Tron bar. They were terrifying affairs; if you lost the audience for even a second they would begin to bay for the gong to be sounded. Whoever was onstage would be immediately ejected! The acts were as eclectic as the audience was brutal. One night a wee old man wearing an Aran polo neck came on with a tap-dancing puppet on a stick. He lifted the puppet to start dancing and everybody immediately shouted 'gong' before the puppet could even get one tap out.

Alan

The gong master was the late, great John Stahl, an actor famous for playing Inverdarroch on *Take the High Road* and who would go on to international fame in *Game of Thrones*. One night backstage at the Tron, as I struggled to make sense of a line during a production of *Macbeth* in which we both appeared, he was also the person who said to me, 'Ach, dae it wi' a look, Alan!' Words of wisdom which I have never forgotten.

Forbes

Victor and Barry not only survived but in fact *won* the Gong Show! A few weeks later we went on win it for a second time before being invited to take part in the Gong of Gongs. This battle of the titans with every one of the show's winners was held in the actual theatre and hosted by Robbie Coltrane, also sadly no longer with us. We won that too!

Alan

That night, little did we know that the Tron would soon become Victor and Barry's home from home, as well as ours. We both acted in various plays there over the next few years and eventually would make our first foray into writing that greatest of all scottish theatrical traditions: panto!

Michael Boyd Remembers...

I was just starting as Artistic Director of the Tron Theatre, and looking for new ways to celebrate Scotland's strong tradition of variety, when Victor and Barry invited me to a soiree of song and conversation. It was to take place at their 'humble home' in the old *AthenaeUM* (their silly emphasis) building of the Royal Scottish Academy of Music and Drama, and I accepted.

Their alter egos, Forbes and Alan, were students there. I was planning a series of variety Gong Nights for the Tron bar, and thought they might fit the bill as a high-end contrast to the precocious 11-year-olds singing 'Girls Just Want to Have Fun', the moothie player, and people hitting their heads with tin trays.

Victor sat at the piano while Barry played the charming frontman, both leading lights of the Kelvinside Young People's Amateur Dramatic Arts Society. They adopted the pretentious air of two mature west-end gentlemen of leisure who dabbled and squabbled, revered Barry Manilow, and played host in their monogrammed dressing gowns. This reassuringly old-fashioned evening, which owed something to Stanley Baxter and a bit to Hinge and Bracket, consisted of several pastiche versions of MOR classics, such as 'Cry Me the Kelvin' and 'Lower Largo Triangle', strung together with patter around the bitter rivalries at KYPADAS.

It was stratospherically camp, wildly cheesy, and could easily have been so-so, but V&B's crazed and genuine investment in their Byres Road torch songs was so brilliantly reflected in their joyous, pitch-perfect delivery. Meanwhile, the developing story of tension between the melancholy piano-bound Victor and the freewheeling egomaniacal Barry was so compelling that it ended up a total triumph. Victor and Barry became the first act to beat the gong at the Tron. Craig Ferguson's *Bing Hitler* was the second, Armando Iannucci the third. Robbie Coltrane was the Gong Master who eventually awarded Victor and Barry the

Gong of Gongs as they triumphed against all other winning acts, including Rex from the Empire Bar on harmonica.

When I commissioned Craig Ferguson and Peter Capaldi to write our first 'alternative' pantomime, *Sleeping Beauty*, Victoria and Barathea were a shoo-in as the perfect Ugly Sisters to torment Beauty. Forbes and Alan went down a storm, and were by now having such success with their double act that I asked them to write the Tron pantomime for the following year. They did so brilliantly and also starred as the eponymous Babes in the Wood.

Meanwhile, Alan played a memorable, haunted Malcolm in our first production of *Macbeth*, and, during rehearsals for *Babes in the Wood*, Forbes played in our ill-fated *Dr Faustus* (or as we called it, The German Play), during which we nearly lost one actor to drink, did lose another to hospital (unable to breathe), and a third, on remand, to HMP Barlinnie. Alan and Forbes wisely refused to begin stage rehearsals for the pantomime until the cabalistic signs that had been painted on our *Faustus* set were removed. Not painted over but completely obliterated by a sanding machine.

Forbes moved the new Tron panto tradition forward with his *Jack and the Beanstalk* and *Cinderella*, while also fitting in his genius *Clov* in *Endgame*, and leads in Tremblay's *The Real Wurld?*, David Kane's *Dumbstruck*, and in our staging of Janice Galloway's *The Trick is to Keep Breathing*.

Victor and Barry eventually became Steve and Sebastian, took off in an aeroplane and never looked back. Until now…

Renee Roberts Remembered

B: We at the Kelvinside Young People's Amateur Dramatic Art Society are the foremost amateur musical company in the whole of Scotland, if not Glasgow.

V: I think Glasgow myself, actually. Yes.

B: And we always endeavor to be that bit different, don't we?

V: Indeed we do. And one year, we decided to branch out into the wonderful, wonderful world of the American musical.

B: Oh, I love them, I love them, I love them, I love them, I love them.

V: They're the bane of my life.

B: That year, we decided to mount that wonderful musical, *Call Me Madam*.

V: Madam! (laughs)

B: You know, it doesn't matter how many times I hear that joke, it still makes me laugh.

V&B: Oh dearie me.

B: But that production was doomed.

V: Thwarted.

B: Pitted.

V: Jinxed.

B: There we were on the opening night at the WRI Hall Kelvinside waiting for the curtains to part, when news filtered through to us that Renee Roberts, who was playing the leading role of the madam, had been involved in a trolley collision in Presto's that day and was unable to take on the role. Of course, as director, I was dumbstruck. Wasn't I, Victor?

V: You were struck dumb.

B: What could I do?

V: I don't know, what did you do?

B: Well, what I did was I stood in the pit and sang the words while Ophelia Wishart, our wardrobe mistress, mimed them on the stage.

V: That's right. I remember you now standing in the pit with your wee dicky bow on. Nothing else, just his wee dicky bow!

B: Stop it. I like it. Victor, of course, was playing the leading male role of Ambrose.

V: A cream of a part.

B: Very rice, very rice.

V: Don't milk it, Barry.

B: I won't.

V: Of course, we've always been highly innovative in our approach to the musical form at Kelvinside, haven't we, Barry?

B: Oh yes, we introduced nudity to Kelvinside in the late '60s. Didn't we, Victor?

V: Yes. It was a production of *Hair*. But unfortunately, due to the age of some of our members…

B: Cast members, I hasten to add.

V: …the trades description people decreed that it couldn't be called *Hair*, it had to be called *Slightly Receding*.

B: And after that, there was a spate of American musicals, wasn't there?

V: Mm-hmm. We did *Calamity Victor*.

B: *Annie Get Your …*

V&B: Uh-huh.

B: But alas, alack, alay, before too long we were to lose our leading lady, Renee Roberts.

V: Renee is a Kelvinside living legend. What's your favourite of her roles, Barry?

B: I think it would have to be that cheese and tomato one she made me in rehearsals.

V: Tsk. It all came about one evening when we were mounting one of our variety spectaculars at the WRI Hall, and Renee was giving her haunting rendition of 'A Nightingale Sang in Blythswood Square'.

B: And there was a star guest in one of our shows; at least he said he was a star. I don't suppose you'll ever have heard of him, a man by the name of Jimmy Logan.

(Victor and Barry pretend to spit on the floor in disgust at the very mention of this name)

V: He lured Renee away from us.

B: The promise of an Equity card, a summer season at Rothesay Pavilion.

V: And the part of the sporran in *The Life and Times of Sir Harry Lauder*.

V; So, this next song is…

V: It's not a song Barry, it's a lament.

B: Yes Victor, it is indeed a lament. A lament for a lost soul. And we would like to dedicate this lament to the memory of Renee Roberts. Hit it, Vic.

V: What, from here?!

V&B: Oh, dearie me!

WE KNEW HER SO WELL

Nothing is so good it lasts eternally, perfect situations must go wrang

But this has never yet prevented us wanting far too much for far too lang

Looking back we could have played things differently (We could have played football)

Done a few more shows who can tell but it took time to understand Renee

       (Who can tell, I do not know)

Now at least we think we know her well

Wasn't she good, she was a wee lamb, wasn't she fabby in Call Me Madame

But in the end she needed a bit more than us, more variety

She ran away with Jimmy Logan, we knew her so well

No one in the company is with us constantly (they come and go, they come and go)

No one stays for long in Kelvinside (I wonder why, I wonder why)

And though we tried our best to keep her, in the end we both broke down and cried

       (we wept!)

Looking back we could have played things differently

       (we could have cast her in other roles)

Learned about Renee before we fell (we were just a little careless)

But Victor was so very much you her then

Now at least we know we knew her well

Wasn't she good, she was no mess, wasn't she magic in Porgy and Bess

Didn't we know, how it would go, if we knew from the start

Why is it we always sing flat? Wasn't she good, wasn't she fine, isn't it madness

She's quit Kelvinside

But in the end she needed a little bit more than us, more variety

She ran away with Jimmy Logan, we knew her so well

We sweated blood and tears to train you, Renee go to hell

1985

LATE 'N' LIVE
POTPOURRI PERFUME
BARCLAY'S BOIL
FIAT 500
EXPLOSIVE EXIT

Forbes

In 1985, we graduated from the RSAMD and entered the big, bad world of showbiz. One of our first professional engagements involved our increasingly constant companions and alter egos, Victor and Barry.

At one of the Tron gong nights the previous year, a woman named Karen Koren had been in the audience. She was about to start programming comedy at McNally's Theatre Club and Restaurant in Edinburgh's Palmerston Place. A man named Brian McNally had originally intended the venue to be a casino, but when he couldn't get a licence from the City of Edinburgh to do so, Karen persuaded him to make it a private members club which put on comedy instead.

Alan

In the spring of 1985, Karen began booking several Scottish acts like *Bing Hitler* (the creation of future US talk show host Craig Ferguson) and the profane magician sensation Jerry Sadowitz, as well as Vic and Baz. At that summer's Edinburgh Fringe, Victor and Barry performed as part of *Late 'n' Live* (it was the '80s: we had an aversion to using the word 'and') whose line-up included Arnold Brown, Paul Merton, Mullarkey and Myers (the latter half of whom was a certain Mike Myers who went on to great things in Hollywood and who, with Paul Merton and Dave Cohen, went on to form The Comedy Store Players in London). Karen, of course, went on to huge success making the Gilded Balloon the epicentre of comedy at the Festival and beyond.

Forbes

The list of denizens who saw Victor and Barry perform that August included comedy icons like Billy Connolly, Lenny Henry and Dawn French as well as April Ashley, the transgender legend who not only attended our show but also returned for McNally's end-of-Festival party.

Alan

I was young and pretty and she flirted with me mercilessly, telling me tales about her many affairs and going to Casablanca in the '60s to have her gender-reassignment surgery. One story ended with a line I've never forgotten: 'Thank god I'm a Baroness in my own right!'

At the end of the afternoon, I was sitting on the steps outside, a little tipsy, and she ran out to a waiting taxi. I waved as she departed and suddenly the taxi stopped and reversed back to me. The window was wound down and an elegant finger beckoned me over.

'Kiss me,' she said. I thought I should do as I was told.

McNALLY'S
THEATRE CLUB
RESTAURANT

APPLICATION
FOR MEMBERSHIP

Name

Address   Age

Just as I leaned in, she said, 'Wait!' and took from her handbag one of those old-fashioned perfume sprayers with the little pump and proceeded to douse herself in fragrance with it.

'Now kiss me!' she ordered. I did. She tasted like potpourri. I stepped back, the window ascended and off she went, leaving me a little wobbly on the pavement.

She died in late 2021, aged 86, and what a life she had. And what a pioneer and trailblazer for trans people, and indeed all of us. And what a good kisser!

Forbes

McNally's was a real upscaling for Victor and Barry. Where previously we had played to drama students and had a few low-level gigs in Glasgow, this felt like we were in with the big boys. The audiences were star-studded, as McNally's was the place to be that year. I remember the night we were told just before we went onstage that Billy Connolly was in the audience; to be in the same room as Billy was a bit of a religious experience for me as I had grown up listening to his records and was a massive fan. To hear him crease himself with laughter at the show was awesome. He came and spoke to us afterwards and told us he had loved it. Such an extraordinary experience.

The Festival run at McNally's boosted Victor and Barry's profile hugely. Suddenly we weren't just a Glasgow secret. It would be a couple of years before the results of this new exposure bore some fruit, but in the meantime there was another development in Victor and Barry's world that we were frankly more concerned with: we got new monogrammed silk dressing gowns.

Alan

Look at us modelling them before one of our sold-out shows in 1985 at the Tron Theatre bar. Please note the extensive set decoration and props involved!

Forbes

The run at McNally's also heralded an art-imitating-life moment for me. Victor and Barry's choreographer at the Kelvinside Young People's Amateur Dramatic Arts Society was Lance Barclay, who'd had a boil in an ana-tomically unfortunate position (true to his name) lanced! Alas, I also fell prey to this sad predicament…

I had not, in fact, graduated from the RSAMD that summer, having failed History of Theatre. I had to re-sit the exam and spent a stressful few weeks swotting prior to Victor and Barry's Festival run. This, combined with the copious drinking which is de rigeur for young performers at the Fringe, perhaps exacerbated the infected pore I contracted after an ill-judged sunbed session which then turned into (you guessed it) a boil. For a couple of shows, a substantial cushion was added to the piano stool to alleviate my discomfort but eventually matters took a turn and we had to cancel two performances to accommodate the inevitable lancing and my recuperation!

Alan

But it was not only Forbes' bum that required repair. I had recently bought a clapped-out, secondhand Fiat 500 which constantly broke down on the trips between Edinburgh and our homes in Glasgow; so much so that I kept a roll of gaffa tape in the back of the car to stick together parts of the engine in order to complete our journey home. We regularly held fish suppers in our laps on the trip for both warmth and sustenance.

Forbes

After McNally's, I got my first professional theatre job at Perth Rep playing John Darling in *Peter Pan* with Rikki Fulton as my dad and Captain Hook. By then, Rikki was an absolute comic legend in Scotland because of his Hogmanay show *Scotch and Wry*, though he was already very famous here as one half of Francie and Jo-sie with Jack Milroy, a double act full of Glasgow patter and songs. My mum and dad were huge fans, and I had seen them when I was wee. In fact, I think we chose the red and blue of our dressing gowns for Victor and Barry because of the colour of Francie and Josie's Teddy Boy

September 17 – October 12, 1985

Peter Pan
by J.M. Barrie

Music and additional Lyrics specially composed by John Scrimger

The Darling Family:

Mr. Darling	Rikki Fulton		
Mrs. Darling	Janet Michael	Michael	Colin McCredie/Michael Diamond
Wendy	Maureen Carr	Nana the Dog	William Elliott
John	Forbes Masson	Liza the Maid	Lesley Moore

The Never-Never Land:

Peter Pan	John Barr	Mermaids:	Cindy Wells
Tinkerbell	Janet Michael		Janet Michael
			Lesley Moore

The Lost Boys:

Slightly	Alan Vicary	First Twin	Colina McCulloch/Paul Byrne
Tootles	Alec Innes	Second Twin	Laura McCulloch/Edmond Byrne
Nibs	Peter Reed	Whirlney	Christopher Asension/Jamie Hayes
Curly	Colin Wojtowitz/Colin Anderson	Bergs	Stephen Antoniewicz/Mark Hampton
		and	
		Captain Hook	Rikki Fulton

Pirates:

Smee	John Ramage	Gentleman Starkey	Iain Stuart-Robertson
Cecco	Ray Dunean	Skylights	David O'Connell
Bill Jukes	Ian Arthur	Mullins	Chico Andradi
Cookson	Tony Ellis	Noodle	Trevor Wood

Indians:

Tiger Lily	Cindy Wells		Iain Stuart-Robertson
Little Panther	William Elliott		David O'Connell
	Hazel Eadie		
	Ray Dunaire		
	Ian		
	Tor		
	G		
	Lu		
	Kir		
	Na		

The Ostrich   Hazel E

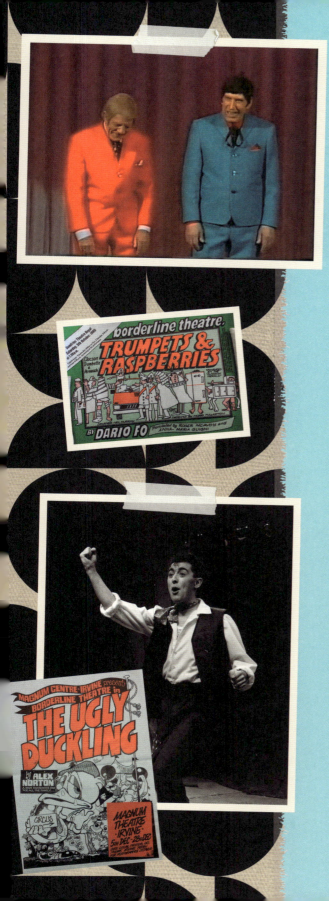

jackets. I also had a kiss curl, in homage to the little tuft that Rikki had in his wig for Josie.

When I met Rikki, he was formidable but very funny, and I learned so much from watching him perform every night. He was very supportive. It was such a buzz to be working with him on my first job. It made my dad's day to meet him, and it was a relief to be able to prove to my dad that I could actually make my way (and some money) as a performer. He was so proud.

In *Peter Pan*, I was playing one of the Darling children and I had to fly. It was a pretty rudimentary effect: they hooked me up in a harness and attached it to a rope. I had to get to a certain position down-stage. Stage manager Gavin Boutcher (Una McLean's son) would pull the rope up and then I would swing ('magically') out the open French windows, off to Neverland.

One night, however, I got in the wrong position; I flew up but crashed into the wall of the set and ended upside down on a chair, before having to get up and walk downstage and try again. The kids in the audience were in hysterics. The musical director was John Scrimger, who had played piano in the amateur production of *Cabaret* I had done in Falkirk. I also discovered that he knew Alan.

Alan

Yes, he helped me with my audition for RSAMD along with Perth theatre associate director Patrick Sand-ford! While Forbes was at Perth, I was on tour with Borderline Theatre Company, working with two other Scottish comedy legends, Elaine C Smith and the late, great Andy Gray in the Dario Fo play, *Trumpets and Raspberries*. It was an amazing experience to watch those two in action, and to see the way the fourth wall could be broken; they also did the 'front of cloth' style that was so prevalent in Scottish theatre but also had its roots in Italian commedia dell'arte. A few years later I would play the Madman in Fo's *Accidental Death of An Anarchist* at the National Theatre in London.

And talking of Borderline, we auditioned together as Victor and Barry for the company's pantomime that year, adapting our 'We're the Boys from Kelvinside' song to suit the occasion, including this epic rhyming couplet:

Where are we? We're at an audition!
We're very big fans of nuclear fission!

Surprisingly, we finished 1985 performing three shows a day as cast members of Borderline's *The Ugly Duckling* by Alex Norton at Irvine's Magnum Centre which is sadly no longer with us. It was a huge leisure complex situated close to what I think was an explosives factory. If there were any safety problems at this factory, the Magnum Centre, needed to be evacuated. Quickly.

The panto was set in a circus. I was a wannabe clown named Andy who befriended the titular duck. Forbes played an evil trapeze artist called Igor Foroffski along with his sister Hedda played by Louise Beattie (daughter of comedian Johnny Beattie) who had been in our year at RSAMD. There was also a character called Signor Bumbaliri who was the Circus Master. His song went, 'Where ere I go they shout yo ho, I Signor Bumbaliri!'

During one matinee we were nearing the end of act two when we saw lights flashing backstage signifying that there needed to be an evacuation. We carried on. Then suddenly we saw two uniformed front-of-house people coming down through the auditorium shouting, 'Stop the show!' We all tried to speed up the ending so the kids in the audience wouldn't be disappointed. Eventually we were all evacuated and huddled around the stage door in our costumes looking cold and miserable with the kids going onto buses while pointing and laughing at us.

There was also an ice rink in the Magnum Centre, and one day between shows we all decided to go for a skate in full costume and make-up. We were not very skilled and most of us fell on our bums. Not exactly Disney On Ice. More wisnae on ice.

Forbes

At the same time as *The Ugly Duckling*, Wildcat was performing their Christmas show *Wild Nights at the Tron* at Glasgow's Tron Theatre. Wildcat was a radical left-wing musical-theatre group born out of John McGrath's 7:84 and led by Dave Anderson and Dave MacLennan. I had been lucky enough to see their shows when I was at school, thanks to a brilliant English teacher called Mr Challinor who used to take us to theatre in Glasgow and Cumbernauld. I saw their

Brechtian show *Dummies* and it blew me away. I had never seen political theatre before. The comedic biting script coupled with the fantastic live rock music was extraordinary. It was one of the things that fired me up to be a professional performer. I wanted to be in such a show.

Wild Nights was a cabaret of their old songs with special guests. The fact that Victor and Barry were considered special enough to be invited onto the bill felt such an honour. We had to rush back from Irvine to perform late in the show. Dave Anderson used to introduce us as 'Glasgow's answer to Hinge and Bracket; a sort of Maryhill Ball and Socket.'

We sang a couple of songs which went down very well with the crowd, then we would get some drinks and go to the back of the auditorium to watch the rest of this fantastic show: Rab Handley singing an anti-festive song ('Christmas time is here, fag end of the year'); Dave Anderson singing an anti-Thatcher song ('Put a woman in power and she'll govern with love/That is what we used to say'); the brilliant guitarist Gordon Dougall who would later become musical director on all my solo work, best man at my wedding, and godfather to my kids. And we both marvelled at the amazing power and talent of singer Terry Neason. We would be seeing more of her in a couple of years.

Karen Koren Remembers...

I put Victor and Barry on at my first venue I ran called McNally's. They were fresh out of the RSAMD. I discovered Victor and Barry performing at the Tron Theatre's *Gong Show*, and asked if they would come and perform at McNally's for the Fringe that year. Their show was hysterical, starting their set with a pastiche of 'Willkommen' from the musical *Cabaret*: instead of singing 'cabaret' they sang 'Vic and Barry'.

At the time, Alan and Forbes were both dating girls they had met at RSAMD. On the last show of that summer of 1985, Hilary Lyon and Kathryn Howden dressed up as Victor and Barry, and did the show pitch perfect. It was hilarious and the boys took it in good part. It was sad when they disbanded as they were a very special partnership and I've been trying to get them to perform at the Fringe ever since. I would still love them to recreate that special charisma they had… even if it was just for one night.

Many years later I was very privileged to be at the press night of *Cabaret* in New York when Alan performed his stunning role of the Emcee. When he sang 'Willkommen', I had 'Vic and Barry' in my head the whole time.

Panto? It's such a drag

THEATRE
By MALCOLM REID

Victor and Barry would like to announce that the transition to Victoria and Barathea has been anything but a drag.

Get yourself along to Glasgow's Tron Theatre before their current outrageous panto production of Sleeping Beauty ends in the next three weeks and I'm sure you will be forced, through tears of laughter, to agree.

Tuning in to the sharply-observed and beautifully-drawn "ugly sisters" routine which Forbes Masson and Alan Cumming execute to hilarious effect as Victoria and Barathea in this "alternative" Christmas show is as easy as falling off a yule log.

Students

Fewer people are aware of the original derivation of this screamingly funny stage twosome.

Forbes (23), from Falkirk, and Alan (21), from Carnoustie, gave birth to Kelvinside's male answer to Hinge and brackett, Victor and Barry, while both were students at Glasgow's Royal Scottish Academy of Music and Drama.

They created the act as part of an entertainment devised to amuse final year students at their going-away thrash and drew on their own personal experiences of some of the worthies they once knew in the amateur theatre to mould them.

"We both grew up in the amateur theatre," explained Forbes, "and

there are the odd few in that field who believe, wrongly, that they are God's gift to acting."

Along the way they threw in shades of Alan's one-time landlady from Kelvinside who used to literally stand at his side with a gushing air freshener as he fried onions in his student flat, and somehow Victor and Barry emerged.

In their dressing gowns, cravats and slicked back hair, Barry (Alan) stands by the piano while Victor (Forbes) tinkles on the ivories and as the pair camp it up and gush about their "careers" with Kelvinside Young Peoples' Amateur Dramatic Arts Society, their finely-honed act induces near-apoplectic laughter among those privileged to have caught the one-hour cabaret number on the fringe theatre circuit.

Theatre buffs love them and those who've enjoyed the act indulge in a kind of one-upmanship over those who've yet to experience it. Performances, as Alan and Forbes reap the benefits of their considerable talent through other

regular acting jobs, tend to be fewer and further apart these days.

There was a time, they realised, when they could probably have made a career out of Victor and Barry.

"Someone wanted to manage us," recalled Alan, "and we were asked to go down to London. But we didn't want to pursue it. We want to stay as Forbes Masson and Alan Cumming, actors in our own right."

"There's also the fear that the act would lose something if we did it full-time," chipped in Forbes. "It might become stale."

"Yes," said Alan, "we feel sort of protective about Victor and Barry. We think to do something like that would be exploiting them in some way."

Catching the act — they've done the last couple of Mayfests and might be featured at this year's — may be harder these days, but the "drag" version, Victoria and Barathea, at the Tron gives a kind of gender-bent flavour of it. Alan and Forbes' talent still shines through the dame make-up.

The pair see Victor and Barry as a sort of hobby, an occasional enjoyable busman's holiday away from the more demanding world of straight acting, they don't try to analyse the success of the act too closely.

"I think a lot of it has to do with Alan and Forbes," said Forbes. "We have a certain rapport with each other.

The strolling players . . . Alan, left, and Forbes

Alan

1986 was a bit of a quiet year for Victor and Barry. It had been such fun and so exciting making up these characters and devising their world, and then to find that people really responded to their weirdness and campery (of course, by that I mean our weirdness and campery!) was wonderful. But then we left college with our day jobs and real lives kicking in, and we kind of left Victor and Barry in dry dock for a while.

Forbes

The act was getting us known to directors in theatre circles, so offers of other work were now coming in. In early 1986, I went back to Perth Rep to be in Joseph and His Amazing Technicolor Dreamcoat. After mocking musicals with Victor and Barry, it felt strange to actually be performing in a real one. While at Perth, they asked

me to join the company for their revival of A Wee Touch o' Class, Rikki Fulton's version of Molière's Le Bourgeois Gentilhomme. I played a stuttering wee flunky: that's me on the left with Rikki and Kenneth Lindsay.

We toured Scotland with this for most of the summer. Rikki was magnetic onstage and always guaranteed to get rounds of applause and raucous laughter for his comedy, but I remember him being worried about taking the show to Perth. I asked him why, and he said that the audiences were much more reserved there, which made him insecure. In one scene, which always stopped the show, it got a smattering of delicate applause from the cool Perth audience. I remember Rikki getting up out of his chair and walking to the front of the stage before sarcastically enquiring into the dark void of the auditorium: 'Oh! Is that the rain on?'

Alan

At the beginning of the year, I was doing a season of plays at the Lyceum in Edinburgh, including a new adaption by Liz Lochhead of Molière's *Tartuffe*.

I remember being in rehearsal for Stuart Paterson's new play *Mr Government* when I got a call from my agent telling me I'd got a big part in *Taggart*. After that, I did another series at STV called *Shadow of the Stone*. Then I experienced soap stardom when I went to *Take the High*

Road (actually it wasn't a soap, but a drama serial, as we were constantly encouraged to refer to it…). I played an evil woodcutter named Jim who arrived in the village of Glendarroch and lodged with Mr and Mrs Blair very shortly after their son Jimmy had died. If you didn't get the message about me being a replacement receptacle for Mrs Blair's maternal feelings, then perhaps the photo of Jimmy on the shelf behind me at their dinner table would have done the trick.

Ironically, later in 1986, Jimmy Chisholm, who had played Jimmy in *Take the High Road*, would feature in the next chapter of Victor and Barry's life!

Forbes

Because Alan and I were both busy on other projects, we had ruled out an Edinburgh Festival excursion for V&B. But then Karen Koren asked us to do a one-off gig at her new Gilded Balloon venue, on a bill with loads of hot new talent from London. Alan had just flown in from somewhere, but his ears hadn't popped from the flight. He could hardly hear anything so the timing of the show suffered. What was meant to be a big showcase for us didn't turn out the best of nights.

Alan

It was a horrible confluence of getting water stuck in my ear from snorkeling on holiday, then the flight exacerbated it. Before I knew it, I was onstage, in pain, doing a show we hadn't done for many, many months, and not able to hear Forbes. It was not V&B's finest hour.

Forbes

We got a call from Michael Boyd, artistic director of Glasgow's Tron Theatre. He was planning to stage a new pantomime, a reinvention of the traditional form, using comedians and writers from the new generation. It was to be *Sleeping Beauty (Young, Gifted & Asleep)* by Craig Ferguson and Peter Capaldi.

Craig had just started to make a name for himself as the comic character *Bing Hitler*. Peter was already a film star, having appeared in Bill Forsyth's *Local Hero*, but I had seen him do stand-up when he was the warm-up act for Spandau Ballet at the Usher Hall in Edinburgh. They wanted us to come on board as ugly sisters. Victor and Barry were to be regendered as Victoria and Barathea, but we had free rein to write our own material and songs.

As a kid I had seen Alastair Sim as Captain Hook at the Alhambra in Glasgow, and Stanley Baxter and Ronnie Corbett as Ugly Sisters at the King's in Edinburgh. I loved the pantomime form, but it had grown tired. This production was going to change all that. It was very funny, dark, surreal and unashamedly Scottish, set in a fantasy land called Vulgaria. There was an evil Doctor Strangelove-esque dentist in an electric wheelchair played by John Stahl. He sang a country and western song called 'It's Good to Be Bad'.

At one point during a banquet scene, he burst out of a

fake fibreglass boar. This was meant to be a show for all the family, but it was so scary that kids were screaming and climbing out of their seats. Craig played the King of Vulgaria and did some of his Bing Hitler routine, and the brilliant Myra McFadyen played the Queen, like a little Glaswegian wifie.

Sleeping Beauty's script was postmodern, punk, progressive and hysterical. The mighty Jimmy Chisholm played Prince Rupert, a sort of thigh-slapping hyperactive Scottish Robin Hood who was searching for the Scone of Destiny. Kay Gallie played a depressed fairy who loved shopping at M&S, and Jake D'Arcy (*Still Game*'s Pete) was a pantomime fly who buzzed about.

With the help of John Stahl, Alan and I wrote this fictional land's national anthem:

God bless Vulgaria
Nation to take care ae ya
Long to reign over ya
You're welcome in Vulgaria

In one scene, Victoria and Barathea said something like, 'Oh this is terrible…I wish we could go on holiday…' which was just an excuse to sing our 'Lower Largo Triangle' song. I remember one performance where the stunning and sorely missed comic genius, Jenny McCrindle (who was playing a gallus Beauty), was meant to be asleep onstage. We were all pretending to be asleep too, around her, when we heard a commotion. The bed she was in had gone on fire, set ablaze by an overheated stage light! Myra rushed on to save her.

Victoria and Barathea's bespoke costumes were a hoot. Alan had a figure-hugging faux fur dress and long dark wig, and I had a camouflage two-piece with pencil skirt and a ginger-bob wig. I had enormous high heels which eventually put my back out from running up and down the stage stairs. When she saw the show, Liz Lochhead, the treasured Scottish poet and dramatist, said that Alan looked like a drag queen and I looked like a lady she knew.

Sleeping Beauty became a huge cult hit and established the Tron Theatre as the home for irreverent and inventive modern pantomimes for decades to come. The Tron was definitely the place to be. It had been an East End church, was rumoured to be haunted, and was now a real hub for Glasgow artists. We all used to stay in the bar after shows, drinking, smoking, laughing, discussing art and theatre, and meeting like-minded souls. It was bohemian and a bit wild. I remember there was a statue in the bar, on loan from the Citizens Theatre while it was being renovated. During one hedonistic lock-in, some people found emulsion and painted it. The next day they were collared and made to clean it all up. I don't think Alan was there, so he is blameless. I, however, had traces of paint under my fingernails…

Alan

We had such a blast doing this show. Our bits were quite self-contained, almost like little comedy routines in themselves, and Peter and Craig were very gracious in letting us contribute our own material. Although we were playing Victoria and Barathea, essentially the Ugly Sisters in panto-speak, they were the essence of Victor and Barry: they still aspired to a world and a class and a gentility that they didn't really belong to and which always somehow eluded them.

I think working together so closely over those few months really got our creative juices going again. It was also perhaps the first time that we realised the power and the freedom of making your own work. We had just left drama school and were now actors for hire, at the mercy of others, waiting for the phone to ring (which luckily it did). But now here we were with something that was not just a fun little sideline we did in late-night clubs for a laugh. Victor and Barry could be our day jobs if we wanted them to be. We could literally make our own work, which we had already been doing during *Sleeping Beauty* without fully realising it. That was a bit of a game-changer, certainly for me, about the possibilities of what we could do together. And within a few months, that awakening became a reality: 1987 became the year of the Victor and Barry explosion!

Bob Clyde Remembers...

I can't remember exactly when I first saw Victor and Barry, but I'll never forget it. As a TV producer, part of my job was to spot new talent. It hardly ever happened. During the Edinburgh Festival, I wandered the closes and wynds, looking for off-piste Fringe venues harbouring undiscovered genius. Most of the time, I came away piste-off or, more likely, just piste. Until that is, I stumbled upon Victor and Barry.

As I recall, the venue was typical Fringe, more morning sickness than Morningside. However, I was immediately struck by the freshness and sophistication of their material. They sent up the send-up, and made it look like they were making it up as they went along. Their act didn't look like an act. They somehow conjured up a world of infectious innocence that drew you straight in. It was a case of art concealing tart. They nearly said the most outrageous things but somehow left us to think of it for ourselves.

We're known as trendy thespians
Some of our best friends are less… well-known
Than us

Or again…
Barry: 'Victor, where's the sex?' [exquisitely timed pause for laugh]
Victor: 'Where they always are, Berry, under the sink'

The first quote is genuine. The second I made up. They're like that. Give it ten minutes, and you're 'doing' V&B! 'Sex' is how they say 'sacks' in the posh parts of Glasgow or Edinburgh. They call the accent pan loaf. But there's nothing plain about Victor and Barry. 'My loaf is a pan; I'm a Kelvin-bred man' went the song, and it's hard to disagree.

Even after 40 years, I still chuckle when I see the old videos and fall straight back into V&B mode, thinking about what they might have said or reacted. How much fun it was to be with their characters and to have a ringside seat at the funfest. And do they actually share a sink? I don't think we ever found out. If only Marigolds could talk…

1987

MAYFEST MUSINGS – FERGUSON FROLICS
CACTUS CAPERS – ASSEMBLY ANTICS

Alan

If making our own work (and living) with *Sleeping Beauty* had given us a glimpse of the freedom and power Victor and Barry could give us, then 1987 quickly proved how difficult it would be to juggle their commitments alongside our acting careers. Looking back on it now, it seems impossible that we did so much Victor and Barry in 1987, and *still* were able to do so many acting jobs too.

In addition to appearing in plays with Dundee Rep, Edinburgh's Theatre Workshop and the Brunton Theatre in Musselburgh (where I had my first brush with the musical *Cabaret*, playing Cliff), I also made a return to *Take the High Road*. There, my evil woodcutter Jim Hunter met a grizzly demise, becoming the first person ever to be murdered in the show, burned alive in Mr Blair's peat shed! Hilariously, when my charred body was recovered from the flames by the polis, STV used an old dummy corpse from *Taggart* to save paying me an extra episode fee!

Everything just sort of exploded that year. Vic and Baz had been our little act that we found hilarious, where we'd get together in one of our flats, have a few drinks then make up a song and laugh our heads off. Now, in what seemed like an incredibly short time, we were hosting all these shows on TV, writing a panto, and meeting and appearing with people we had, until very recently, idolized from afar. At the time we were so young and hungry, and it was incredibly exciting and kind of surreal for all these opportunities to come our way. But reflecting on it now, I remember just how overwhelming it was. Amazing, but overwhelming. We just sort of clung on to each other and went along for the ride!

Forbes

After the hedonistic Christmas at the Tron for *Sleeping Beauty*, Michael Boyd asked us if we would like to write a new Victor and Barry pantomime. We started thinking of ideas. In the meantime, I stayed for more craziness at the Tron to work with the then Associate Director, Hamish Glen, playing a young Hussar in Chris Hannan's version of *Gogol's Gamblers*, which played both the Tron and Traverse.

I also managed to find time to film the part of a suspicious hotel manager, a red (haired) herring in *Taggart*. Alan went off to Dundee Rep to play Phil in John Byrne's *Slab Boys*, but it wasn't long before Victor and Barry were back in the frame.

"Take The High Road"
Alan Cumming
as
JIM HUNTER

SCOTTISH TELEVISION

Alan

The madness began when we got a call from Bob Clyde, a producer at Scottish Television. He had come to see us at McNally's Theatre Club in 1985 and told us that he loved Victor and Barry and would be in touch. Well, it took 18 months but he was true to his word, so in early '87 he asked if we'd be into hosting some bits after the six o'clock news during Mayfest, Glasgow's annual international arts festival which ran from 1983 to 1997. We said YES!

Forbes

We did three shows a week during the three-week festival, averaging about five minutes per appearance. Each episode had clips of Mayfest highlights including plays from South Africa, a Spanish company performing *The Mikado* (in Catalan), a Chinese acrobat and plate-spinning troupe, and Scotland's own *Merry Mac Fun Show*. Because there was so much information to convey about who and what to see, and because we also tried to infuse all this information with some Vic and Baz-style pizazz into a short burst, we had to talk incredibly quickly to stuff everything in. There was one sequence where Victor and Barry were talking about shows that Alan and Forbes were doing as themselves. I was in a play called *Getting Past It* by Lynn Bains, playing Elaine C Smith's young lover.

Alan

Monday the 4th of May, 1987, was like any other spring day in Scotland. The skies were calm(ish), there were a few showers and it got a bit nippy later on. Who knew that at 6.35pm all our lives would be changed forever?

For that was the day Victor and Barry were propelled onto the screens and into the hearts of an unsuspecting Scottish TV-watching public when *A Guide to Mayfest with Victor and Barry* made its auspicious debut…

45

A Guide to MAYFEST

with Victor and Barry

Victor is humming Take the High Road's theme tune and hoeing a flower bed outside Kelvingrove Art Gallery. Barry approaches, driving a very large vintage car along the pavement. Both are wearing the prototype V&B look: very large dressing gowns made from old unwieldy curtain material, cravates and slippers.

Barry: Victor! Victor!
Victor: What is it? Can't you see I'm busy?
B: Guess who I've just had on the phone?
V: Oh no, not Roy Hudd asking about margarine again?
B: No! Scottish Television!
V: Really?
B: Yes, they want us to present a series of nine programmes during Mayfest entitled A Guide to Mayfest with Victor and Barry!
V: Well, I never!
B: Uh huh!
V: What's the money like?

B: Well, it's sort of blue with pictures of the Queen on it.
V: No, don't be stupid. How much are we getting?
B: Oh, the usual Scottish Television fee, you know?
V: Well, we could do with a new hoe...
B: Mmhmm.

(They arrive in the Scottish Television studio)

Victor: So, I said, fresh? You're well before the sell-by date!

(They guffaw and take in their surroundings)

B: Oh! So, this is the kernel of the nut that is Scottish Television, is It?
V: It's a lot smaller than you think.
B: I wonder how they get his place to look like Loch Lomond?

(He suddenly gasps as he looks over to see the Scotland Today host, Alan Fisher, collecting his papers after finishing the news broadcast)

B: Victor! Is that not that newscaster over there?
V: Yes, well I must say, Sheena McDonald looks a lot different in the flesh, doesn't she?

(Victor is now sitting at a piano, Barry leaning atop it. They have ear pieces in and are awaiting instructions from their unseen director, Lance)

V: Oh, it's a Steinway! They might have tuned it.
B: Well, we're ready, Lance! For goodness' sake, you wouldn't need to be in a hurry, would you?
V: Well, I *am* as a matter of fact. Because I want to go and see the world premiere of *The Sleep* at the Mitchell Theatre tonight.
B: *The Sleep*? What's that?
Victor: It's a highly ambitious and innovative work about a woman who has been locked into a dream state for 40 years.
B: That sounds gripping!
V: And it stars Sarah Jane Morris from The Communards.
B: Well, I want to go along and see the late-night cabaret at the Mayfest Club in Moir Hall tonight.
V: Who's on?
B: Well, it's a star-studded evening. There's Elaine C Smith, David Anderson, Gavin Meechie, Rollin' Joe and The Sirens.
V: I feel a song coming on.

B: Well, I've got a few lyrics up my sleeve! Hit it, Vic!
V: What, from here?!

(They both laugh)

B: A wan, a two, a wan two three four!
V&B singing: *It's that time of year once more!*
Switch aff the video, don't be a bore
Go get some culture, grab what's yours
V: *You won't have seen things like this before*
V&B: *Let off some steam, get it aff yer chest*
To see better shows you'd be hard pressed
So come along with us and we'll show you the best
Vic and Barry's Guide to... Mayfest!
B: Was that alright, Lance?
V&B: What do you mean you don't like the number?
B: We'll be back on Wednesday, just after *Scotland Today*. Don't miss it.

****

Victor and Barry dancing in George Square, wearing sweatbands on their heads and one leg warmer each. They are still speaking incredibly quickly.

V&B: Hello there, fans!
V: Welcome to the second installment of our Mayfest guide! And as youse have probably guessed, tonight's programme is devoted to dance!
B: Yes, it's Victor and Barry's Mayfest dance special!

V: And in commemoration of this I have been up all night with my knitting needles and I have knat these lovely leg warmers…

(They stick out a leg each to display said item)

V: Unfortunately, I ran out of wool.
B: But they're very nice, very sturdy, very practical! Tonight's show is really energetic!
V: Oh! I'm worn out just looking at the guest list.

B: Well, we're really getting the hang of this TV presenting lark, Victor. If I'm not mistaken that is what is known in the business as a link!
V: What, you mean like a sausage?

(Later, Victor displays his mime skills in front of dancers from Scottish Dance Theatre in Kinning Park…)

****

V: Hello there, fans!
B: Greetings viewing millions! And what a stoatir of a show we've got lined up for youse tonight! Haven't we, Vic?!
V: Yes!
B: *(to the viewers)* Oh you've hoovered the carpet!
V: But have you seen the state of that screen? It's absolutely clairty!
B: It is a bit manky in the corner there.
V: Anyway, we're nearing the end of the first week of Mayfest, Glasgow's own international festival of the arts.
B: And what a week it has been! Victor and Barry have become internal cogs in the Scottish media machine!
V: In fact, we have been inundated with a letter from Mrs B of Pollokshields.
B: Who writes...
V: Dear John, could you return the library book on pre-Byzantine origami?
B: Have you seen your optician recently, Mrs B?

B: That's it for tonight you culture vultures!
V: You arty anchovies!
B: This is Victor and Barry saying…
V: Goodnight Scotland!

****

(We see Victor and Barry driving their Humber towards us in some wasteland beneath the Finnieston Crane that is probably now home to an eaterie that serves vegan haggis pakora

and its ilk. We hear them talking about the fallout from the general election announcement two days prior)

B: So, I said 'the next time you decide to have an election, make sure you have it after Mayfest, because our programme had to be put back to 11.30!'

(They get out of their car to see people in business suits walking around and one of them is writhing in agony on the ground)

V: What in the name of Jimmy Logan is this?
B: This is what we theatricals call street theatre, Victor, and it's where the artistes actually perform in the street.

****

(Barry blows a raspy note through a tuba)

B: Oh! In the name of Joan Burnie, I'm puffed!
V: Are you peched?
B: They make us do everything on this show, you know!

V: Slave drivers!
B: And all for the price of a new big end for our Humber.
V: Anyway, welcome to tonight's show, ladies and gentlemen.
B: Hello fans!
V: Or as we say at the Mayfest Club…
V&B: Hello darling, mine's a double gin!
B: We've had another letter from Mrs B of Pollokshields (remember her?) who writes…
V: Dear John, as regards our telephone conversation, my answers are yes, no, gas regulo 5 and rubber gloves.
B: Get a grip, Mrs B!

****

(We find Victor and Barry closing the bonnet of their Humber outside the Third Eye Centre on Sauchiehall Street)

V: So, she said, 'lasagne alfresco with a fish?!'
B: Never! For goodness' sake!
V: So, this is the Third Eye Centre, eh?
B: I wonder what happened to the other two?!

V: I spy with my little third eye somebody beginning with Liz Lochhead!

(Barry thinks for a long moment)

B: Jim Kelman!
V: Correct.

(Victor and Barry are now inside the Third Eye Centre finishing off a snack in the café)

V: Another cup of tea, Barry?
B: Are you kidding? I'm stuffed. It's a bit parky in there, isn't it?
V: My teeth are chattering.
B: Well, why don't you take them out and put them in a glass of hot water? Ha! Only kidding Victor, I know they're all your own. You made the final payment last week. (to camera) Oh hello there, fans, how are you?
V: Here we are in the café of the Third Eye Centre.
B: Home to artistic Glaswegians of all ages.
V: No doubt you've just finished your meal. What was it? Oh no, not mince again?
B: Why, oh why, can't you be more adventurous in the kitchen?
V: We just had beansprout casserole with Possilpark prawns.
B: And very tasty they were too.
V: Barry, is that not that actor Alan Cumming over there?
B: You know, I think it is. That boy has never been the same since Take the High Road.
V: Still carries a chainsaw in his car, I believe.
B: Shh! Well, the place is fair hoaching with celebs today, isn't it?
V: Mmm... there's Elaine C Smith of Naked

Video fame over there.
B: Who's that strange wee chap with the red hair sitting next to her?
V: I don't know but his face is strangely familiar.
B: Och I know! It's Forbes Masson the actor; or so he says!
V: He's emergent apparently.
B: So, I've heard. Oh Victor, I don't feel very well.
I think it was those Possilpark prawns.
You know what my tummy's like.
V: Yes. Fat!
B: Oh, that's it. Laugh at my discomfort. I'm off to buy some Setlers.
V: I'll just have a word with George Wyllie while you're away.
B: Well, just you do that.

****

V: (whispering to camera) It's George Wyllie!

(He approaches George who has been studying a painting)

V: George Wyllie... I can call you George, can't I?
George: Certainly.
V: Pleased to meet you.
G: Very polite.
V: Now there's been something I must ask you: what on earth possessed you to stuff a locomotive with straw?
G: Well, it wasn't so much the locomotive, it was the crane.
V: The Finnieston Crane?
G: The Finnieston Crane. And the locomotive I decided to hang on the crane; and having

decided that, I decided to stuff the locomotive full of straw.

V: It reminds me of that time I stuffed a tram full of raffia… much more colourful… and not so much of a fire hazard.

****

(Victor and Barry drive up to the Tron Theatre in their Humber)

B: So, I just turned round and said to her, 'I've never seen tomatoes stuffed like that before.'

V: She never changes, does she?

B: Oh, hello there viewing millions!

V: Hello fans! And welcome to our final installment [wipes away a tear]. Sad, isn't it? And here we are at the Tron Theatre.

B: Yes, we remember it when it was a church.

V: It's a nice place. At least it will be when it's finished.

B: Well, that's nearly what Mayfest is, you know.

V: A church?

B: No, finished.

(Later we find Victor and Barry in the Tron bar, as Barry receives a message in his imaginary earpiece...)

B: What is it, Lance?

V: What does he want now?

B: For goodness' sake, why did you not tell us that before?

V: What?

B: Well, apparently they've had a phone call from the producer of Crossroads. Their ratings are very poor at the moment.

V: I'm not surprised. Have you seen that programme?

B: And they want us to sing a song just before Crossroads comes on.

V: Why?

B: Well, the last time we sang a song the ratings trebled. I think they want to catch our audience.

V: So, we sing a song and people watch Crossroads?

B: Yes, I think so.

V: What's it worth?

B: A free weekend in Birmingham and the chance to see an episode of Crossroads being recorded.

V: Oh, that should be good for a laugh.

V&B SING:

It's over, goodbye friends
C'est finit, it's the end
The party's over, it's the end of the line
This is a new sentence
One of us is singing out of time
[Barry: And it's not me]
We did it our way, no regrets
C'est lavvy, good things must come to an end

(Victor embarks on some increasingly loud vocal riffs as Barry talks to the viewing millions.)

B: Well fans, we hope you've enjoyed our Guide to Mayfest here on Scottish Television. We certainly have. And we hope that before too long we'll be back with you in your living rooms, your bedrooms, your kitchens, your toilets or wherever you keep your televisions.

(He is barely audible now and finally snaps)

Shut up, Victor! But in the meantime…

V&B SING: We've been to Mayfest
Now we're going home to Kelvinside!!

(They both burst into tears)

V&B: Give us another job Gus, please!

(Gus Macdonald was the then head of Scottish Television).

Forbes

We also performed as Victor and Barry onstage at the Tron and Third Eye Centre during Mayfest, and late night at the Mayfest Club, a boozy smoky hang-out with all the artists at that year's festival. I remember thinking we had gone up in the world, now that we were mixing socially with all the Wildcat performers I had admired while I was at school. We were alongside John Sparkes who had a character called Siadwel on BBC's *Naked Video*, and went on to become one of the voices on *Peppa Pig*. We also met the sensational Arnold Brown again.

For one night at the Glasgow Pavilion, we teamed up with Craig Ferguson as Bing Hitler, plus Craig's sister Lynn Ferguson, and Carolyn Bonnyman who had been the year below us at drama school and had formed the very funny Alexander Sisters.

In June, *The List* were becoming aware of our increasing popularity so we did a big interview for the magazine, and they made us cover stars.

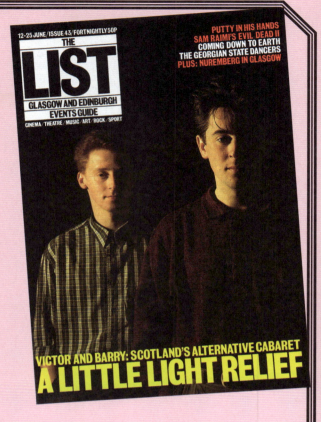

Alan

We did a show at the Tron where we tried out some new material. We did a parody version of the old Dean Martin song 'You're Nobody Till Somebody Loves You'. One of the lines in that song was 'the world still is the same, you never change it'; as there was a General Election around the corner, we added 'not even by tactical voting'.

Another try-out was the song 'No Two People (Have Ever Been So in Love)' from the old Danny Kaye movie *Hans Christian Andersen*, though we augmented the title to 'No Two People (Have Ever Been So in Love with the Theatre as Us)'. At a crucial point in the song, Barry held up a can of Heinz Beans and a spool of thread. Bean. Sew. Get it? No? Neither did anyone else, so we cut it.

We did a version of Terry Jacks' 'Seasons in the Sun' but we changed the lyrics to 'we had joy, we had laughs, we had bubbles in our baths'. It went down the plughole. And then there was a Kelvinside version of 'Can't Help Lovin' Dat Man' from the musical *Show Boat* which we changed to 'Can't Help Savin' Those Green Shield Stamps'. It didn't stick. We decided that the time for parodies was over and that we really should be writing more original material. With this in mind, we had a meeting with Michael Boyd and decided on *Babes in the Wood* as our Tron panto. We started writing both the show and some original songs for it.

Forbes

I also got the small part of Crawford Minty in BBC Scotland sitcom *City Lights* and got to work for the first time with the much missed and dearly loved Andy Gray. Because of the success of our Mayfest shows, Scottish Television asked us to be the in-house comics and script writers/editors on a new TV show filming in July at The Gateway in Edinburgh. It was to be a vehicle for the extraordinary Scottish actress and singer, Terry Neason, the Wildcat diva we had first met in 1985.

We started work on writing the links for her show, and initially we were given a free rein to do as we pleased. We wanted to capitalise on Terry's uniqueness, and her tough, Glasgow comic sensibility. We wanted her to use her own catchphrase ('how's it hingin?') but the powers balked at that and thought it was too rude. It soon became clear that STV were trying to push Terry in another, more safe direction. A softer, light-entertainment route.

We were also quite disheartened when we were more or less told that our ambitions for this to be shown on the UK network were unrealistic, and there was no point even trying and not to bother. It felt so defeatist. We were really proud of our Scottish voice and wanted to push for it to be heard nationwide, but they

It is no secret that Scottish Television have been looking for a new light entertainment format with which to hit not just Scottish audiences but to mount an assault on the network. This could be the programme – certainly it boasts a wealth of talent (much of it new to television) drawn from the Scottish theatre and music circuits.

Following the structure of good old fashioned TV variety shows, a singer, Terry Neason forms the pivot of the six show series. Sometime singer with Wildcat, she's a big lady with a strong voice who scored a popular hit with her portrayal of Eva Peron. She's joined on the new show by Victor and Barry – one of the hottest comedy properties around – and some of the current crop of successful Scottish bands. Hue and Cry, and Deacon Blue amongst others are scheduled to appear and Hank Wangford, not long since departed from Acropolis Now will also be popping in. Can Scottish Television reinvent the variety show for the eighties? (N.B.)

20 The List 18 Sept – 1 Oct

thought we were cocky young pups. It was not to be.

Still, the show was a big hit on STV and we did have a great laugh working with Terry. Victor and Barry were given a makeover. Gone were the dressing gowns and in came the monogrammed blazers and cream slacks. They kept the cravates though. We also had Susie Maguire playing various comic characters, including a fine version of Muriel Gray. It was exciting to be in the TV studio working alongside such great Scottish bands and singers like Hue and Cry, Deacon Blue, Danny Wilson, Tam White and the Dexters, Myra McFadyen, and Elaine C Smith. And Terry herself blew it out of the park. There were other comics, too, including a very young Paul Merton doing some stand-up, in crutches as he had a broken leg and was in a stookie!

Alan

One of the things I've found amazing about looking back at our Vic and Baz days is the amount of crazy things I had totally forgotten about. I know it was a long time ago, and we did pack in an incredible amount of work in a very short time both writing and performing, but I was pretty shocked to realise I'd totally forgotten that I had once played a cactus! Or more precisely, I played Barry as a cactus in a dream of Victor's!

(*Victor and Barry are in their dressing room. They have make-up smocks over their outfits and as they chat, they perform various acts of personal toilette: eyebrow grooming, ear cleaning, puffing on an inhaler, examining their teeth etc. Victor has a kirby grip keeping his kiss curl in place. Over the loud- speaker they hear Terry and the audience in the studio below. She becomes more raucous and the audience more hysterical with laughter as the scene continues.*)

Terry: Unfortunately, Victor and Barry won't be able to join us tonight due to a stroke of genius on my part. No, only kidding, due to an industrial dispute.

Barry: So, I just said to her...
Victor: Who? Terry?
B: Uh-huh! Terry Neason. I said, 'You'll re- gret it, Terry!'
V: Regret what?
B: Regret the fact she doesn't want to do a number with us.
V: Really?
B: Uh-huh! She said she wouldn't be seen dead singing with Victor and Barry and that we were a couple of tone-deaf, am-dram has-beens!
V: Well, that's ridiculous because we know people would give their teeth to sing with us.
B: Exactly! So, I just said to her, 'Terry, my good lady, unless you apologise for those remarks, Victor and I will refuse to appear on tonight's show.'
V: That was putting it in her pipe. Did she smoke?
B: Well, she was jumping up and down with disappointment.
V: Yes, I thought that cheering I heard sound- ed a bit anxious. So, what exactly is our method of recourse?
B: Well Victor, we just wait here until Terry comes up and apologises before we deign to go down to the studio floor.

(*A pause. Terry delivers another punchline and the audience cracks up.*)

B: She'll be here any minute.

(*Another pause. More guffaws from below.*)

B: I'm sure of it.

(*A little later…*)

V: …a gruyère cheese quiche and a handy holdall.
B: Right! Ms Cranston went to the delicatessen and bought an avocado, a bottle of Perrier, cucumber cleansing milk, a…
V&B: …doner kebab-flavoured dip.
B: An egg timer.
V: Yes, that was mine.
B: A gruyère cheese quiche, a handy holdall and…an Icelandic prawn bap!

V: No, no! You're out! You forgot F for
fancy fondant.
B: Oh rats!
V: So that's two Camparis and three packets
of cashew nuts you owe me now, Barry!

(A silence.)

V: Do you think we should go down to the studio now?
B: Certainly not, Victor. I mean, there's no
point in causing a fuss and then climbing down
from your pedestal, is there?
V: No.

(Later still. Victor is asleep, wearing a
blue-gel eye mask and lightly snoring. Barry
is hitting the Campari. There's a knock at
the door.)

B: See? That'll be her now, begging with for-
giveness. Come!

(We cross fade to a desert backdrop. Terry
is dressed as a Native American. Victor as a
Canadian Mountie. They're doing a duet of an
old Nelson Eddy and Jeanette MacDonald hit…)

T: When I'm calling you-ooh-ooh-ooh-ooh-
ooh-ooh.
V: (it's a little high for him; we'd nowadays
call him a little pitchy) I will answer too-
ooh-ooh-ooh-ooh-ooh-ooh-ooh.

(They begin to sidle romantically towards each
another but their progress is impeded by a
cactus that pokes Terry in the hand with
one of its spines. Victor begins kissing it
better. We now see the cactus has a face:
it's Barry's, and he keeps repeating
Victor's name.)

B: Victor! Victor!

(We are back in their dressing room)

B: Victor! Wake up, Victor!

(Barry rips off the eye mask and Victor jolts
awake. He's kissing his own hand.)

V: What is it?
B: It's the security man at the door. We've
got to vacate the dressing room. Everyone's
gone home.
V: You mean it was all a dream?

Forbes

We had been contacted by William Burdett-Coutts who ran (and still runs) Assembly in Edinburgh during the Fringe. I think he had seen us at McNally's and invited us to come and perform for about two weeks in the Edinburgh Suite, which was the smallest venue there. We decided to try something different and have both of us sing away from the piano, so we recorded a backing track. The idea was that Andrew Lloyd Webber had been in our amateur company and had stolen our ideas, so we performed several parody songs. I asked Eddie Jordan, a friend I'd met at Perth Theatre, to record the backing track. He is a member of Scottish band Fiction Factory who had a huge hit in 1983 with '(Feels Like) Heaven'.

It was very exciting to be in the Assembly Rooms as it was pretty much the focal point of the Edinburgh Fringe then. It was actually very unusual for local performers to perform there. We got quite a mixed audience of locals and tourists, and the shows sold very well. One of our fans was a young Kathy Burke, who was up there performing and saw our show a couple of times.

We were asked to perform late night at the Fringe Club which had a raucous audience full of late-night revelers. We also were asked on to Brian Matthew's *Round Midnight* on Radio 2. Brian was a very popular DJ, had been successful since the 1950s, and was a big fan of V and B. He used to like it when Victor and Barry referred to his wonderful products (confusing him with Bernard Matthews, the turkey king).

Ode to Andrew

Victor: We'd now like to tell you about a Judas we had in our midst at the Kelvinside Young People's Amateur Dramatic Arts Society.
Barry: Indeed, a young man who was our assistant musical director for many, many years, who then left us and went on to bigger and better things, stealing some of our best ideas for shows!
V: A man by the name of Andrew Lloyd Webber. Heard of him? Listen to the titles of some of these shows and see if you've heard them somewhere before…Victor and his Amazing Multi-textured Cardigan.
B: Sound familiar, ladies and gentlemen?
V&B: We think it does!
B: Or how about the show concerning the rise to fame of a man with amazing powers entitled Jimmy Logan Superscot!
V: It's got the same number of letters.
B: Exactly!
V: And what of the musical about the South American dictator who was slimming…Ryvita!
B: Sound an eeksie peeksie bit familiar? Then there was the show when we branched into surrealism…
V: We branched, we branched, yes.
B: …a show about a set of traffic lights in Kelvinside that had remained at red for over 20 years entitled Traffic Lights Repressed.

It's a slow burn… think about it later.
V: But the worst crib of all, and the most recent, was The Bogey of the Musical.
B: Heard that somewhere before? And so now, as we reach the witching hour (five past nine), we would like to summon the spirits of those shows past and wreak our revenge on this cruel, cruel cribber.

Victor and Barry start to sing a song that bears a striking resemblance (though for copyright reasons not that striking) to 'Any Dream Will Do' from Joseph and the Amazing Technicolor Dreamcoat.

He started off with a bible story,
now he's a rampant Tory
Any tune will do
He makes his cash from plagi-thingmy
He's a cheeky wee bizzum
So, Andy, we're going to copy you
[Spoken]: It's dead easy

This next part sounds a bit like 'Don't Cry for Me Argentina!'

So don't tell us you're innovative
We've heard that chord sequence before
It was in your last show, and the one before that
And the one before that one, and it's probably in the one you're writing at the moment

Now back to 'Any Dream Will Do'

He knows the score, he got rid of Tim
Then he wrote a song in Latin, called 'Pia
Uh Jayzooo'
Tim's fighting back (Tim's fighting back)
He's a money grabber (Ah Ah Ah)
So, he wrote a show with ABBA (AhAhBah)
Any words will do
He's as bad as Andrew
Any tune will do

The next bit sounds like 'Memory' from Cats

Amnesia, he thinks we've got amnesia
Andy, we don't believe ya, we've heard it
all before
We remember when Sarah Brightman danced in
underwear

No, our memories aren't that short

This bit is like 'All I Ask of You' from Phantom of the Opera

It's so boring cos we know what comes next
Yes, it's that same bit again
Any tune will do

For the finale we hear a Phantom theme derivative...

In dreams he comes to us, we hear his shows
We wake up sweating in case he knows
That we're try-ing to be Andrew Lloyd
Webber
Yes, we would like to be Andrew Lloyd
Webber
But we're not
[Spoken] We're not!

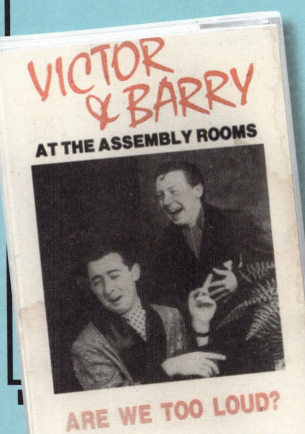

Alan

During our run at the Assembly Rooms, we recorded one live show and released it as an album entitled *Are We Too Loud?*

We also appeared on the BBC's *Combing the Fringe* and on STV's *Acropolis Now*.

On both occasions we sang our new composition 'The Edinburgh Festival Song', which bore a startling similarity to a road safety public information film from the 1960s. The one where the little boy said, 'This is my nan, she always waits there', and 'It was my dad! In a new car!'

Victor: This is a public information song

Edinburgh Festival, it's the one that's best of all
You can do a show in an old scout hall in Stockbridge
Do an all-nude version of a Chekhov play
Or juggle with spears of broccoli
Or play the French dressing in Salad Days
You can be theatrical for three weeks.

Edinburgh Festival, it's the one that's best of all
If you're an actor resting, call your agent
Cos there will be a part somewhere
In the stage adaptation of Dr Kildare
Or a musical version of Where Eagles Dare
Or something rude in the open air
You can be theatrical for three weeks.

Be arty, go to after-show parties
Talk about commedia dell'arte
Maybe meet Russell Harty
V: if you're lucky!
See the Tattoo, read The Scotsman reviews
Stand all day in a que-hue
Trying to get tickets for Victoria Wood
V: But she's sold out.

B: Slow things down a bit Victor, I feel a ballad coming on.
V: Do you?
B: Yes.

The culture vultures are never seen without their Fringey brochures
They try to see ten shows a day, nine of which are atrocious
The pubs are busy, the town's in a tizzy, the weather isnae hot
And why is it so difficult to meet someone who's Scottish?

V: The place is like an Oxbridge ghetto.
B: Exactly! Viva Caledonia!

Be arty, go to after-show parties
Talk about commedia dell'arte
Maybe meet Russell Harty
V: Why bother?
See the Tattoo, read The Scotsman reviews
Stand all day in a que-hue
B: Still trying to get tickets for Victoria Wood.
It's a waste of time.

Edinburgh Festival, in this city east of Falkirk and Glasgow!

they do"
"and that's what's quite odd at the moment because Victor and Barry are becoming celebrities in their own right. the whole point of the act was that they thought they were celebrities so there's this strange..."
"and so now we've got a new song and it's called 'It's Hard Being a Celebrity' because they are quite within the kind of trendy, alternatively set, they are quite celebrities. Before, they were the leading lights of Kelvinside and now they're going for mass media. Media personalities, that's what they're calling themselves. So it's quite funny the way we've had to alter the act because of the increasing fame of it, if you like."
"Yes, and the characters themselves are changing. For the Terry Neeson Show they are not...even the look of the characters is changing, they're becoming more smooth, sophisticated, but I think that's something that's necessitated by Terry. Our stage act is very different, because on TV we're just being zany presenters, we do numbers and such like but basically we're there as a silly presence. The raunchiness of the stage act you can't reproduce on telly, the medium of telly means that you have to be, you have to look smoother."

"They always knew they would end up on Scottish Television..."
"They had to be begged you know, oh yes."
"Letters from Gus McDonald, they're not easy, they're no pushover, so it took them a while, they had to be asked on several occasions and, of course they're taking it in their stride. They're learning..."
"Sex and violence and ego massage. As we get more sure of ourselves they are saying more and more...political things. I think Victor and Barry are becoming more dangerous as we are becoming more secure."
"The Hinge and Bracket thing's been around for ages and it's understandable because they are quite...the stage act is very musically based and it's twee and"
"It's camp"
"and it's camp and it does look ...
"the Pete and Dud thing's come up a couple of times but that's more on telly because we do have things not to camera. You can understand where these comparisons come from but there is no real parallel because our stuff is original, I mean we don't feel any particular influence. The good thing is that we have known Victor and Barry a long time, they've been on the go for"
"Five years, now."
"five years. So the thing is that we don't need any influences."
"It would be very easy for us to let Victor and Barry go on for ever, but are both, as individuals, getting more work as actors in our own right : that's good. We'll keep on as long as possible with Victor and Barry. T came from people we saw, yes, in amateur dramatics, but not anyo particular. Victor and Barry are so outrageous, I don't think there are like that...I hope not...but amateur people should not be offended, and Barry are not patronising, they aren't there to take the pis amateur dramatics, there are lots of good people in amdram who tak seriously and do very good work. Victor and Barry are larger tha they are quite sad in a way because they are hanging on to thi doesn't exist. I think there's a quandary approaching for Victo because they are getting famous."
"As a nation we are really hung up about our Scottishness recently that there has come about a sort of pride in it...it's ji that is a national trait. I mean they said that they couldn't und Frutti', but can you understand half of what Den says or Victor and Barry epitomise that national trait, the Scots infer That's changing, so Victor and Barry are, i___ "

ALAN CUMMING AND FORBES MASSON, LIFELONG FRIENDS WORLD FAMOUS THESPIANS VICTOR McILVANEY AND BARR McLEISH, REPORT ON THE LATEST MEDIA COUP: SCOTTIS TELEVISION'S TERRY NEESON SHOW. JIM WAUGH POURE THE COFFEE, GERRY McCANN TOOK THE B&Ws.

"Victor and Barry are two ageing would-be thespians

Alan

Because of the exposure from our *Guide to Mayfest* and *The Terry Neason Show*, Scottish Opera asked us to be part of an ad campaign. We were to advertise their new production of Alban Berg's *Lulu*. I seem to remember Victor and Barry actually going in costume to a performance. We met and had a great laugh with the Scottish Opera music director, the great John Mauceri, and both of us would later work with him individually: Forbes soon with Scottish Opera, and me many years later making my solo concert debut at the Hollywood Bowl!

Forbes

In October, maximising on the success of *The Terry Neason Show*, we supported her at a one-off performance at Glasgow's Pavilion Theatre.

Alan

As the year careered to a climax, we hosted STV's *Victor and Barry's Scottish Review of the Year*, which began with our heroes in their lounge (it was actually producer Bob Clyde's bijou West End residence) decorating their Christmas tree, with Barry admonishing Victor for over-imbibing in the chocolate Santas: 'A moment on the lips, a lifetime on the hips,' he quipped.

Then they began to examine the presents under their tree...

V: Who's that one for?
B: That's for Viola Tuck, our next-door neighbour.
V: What is it?
B: It's a cleaning kit for her hearing aid.
V: Pardon?
B: It's a cleaning kit for her hea...
(They dissolve into laughter)
B: What's that one there?
V: Oh, that's for our butcher, Ruari Blacklaws.
B: I didn't know we gave to him.
V: Well, he's very generous with his giblets.

They then open a gift from Scottish Television. It's not the cheque they were hoping for, but instead it's a VHS tape of STV's greatest hits of that year. Of course, they presume it will be packed with footage of them, and so they proceed to watch and comment between the clips, resulting in, hey presto, another half hour of television gold! One of the actual shows in there was the reunion of Rikki Fulton and Jack Milroy's Francie and Josie at the King's Theatre in Glasgow.

Peter Pans and their stardust melodies

Victor and Barry: That's the Way It Is Tuesday 29 December 8.55 Radio Scotland

ON STAGE, consciously soigné in their matching silk dressing gowns and insouciant cravats, they inhabit a world of stardust melodies. To their faithful audiences, this musical duo from Glasgow's Kelvinside is unparalleled.

Yet for Victor and Barry, widespread recognition of their peculiar talents has proved elusive. Opportunities never panted up the endless flights of stairs to their Kelvinside attic, hoping to find them. Inevitably, however, I did.

Offstage, Victor MacIlvaney and Barry McLeish are intensely private people. They also look smaller. Courteously they usher me into the kitchen. 'You must forgive the informality, Mary. Barry was quick to put me at my ease – but we're having the dining room redecorated. Our fee for this BBC documentary has just come through – unfortunately it hasn't quite covered all the walls.'

The truth, as I discover, is that only the excess boasts the covered vinyl embossed wallpaper. To them, however, the room is not half unfinished, it is half complete.

While we wait for Barry – he's the cook of the household – to boil the kettle, I study the walls. Hung over with memorabilia of their career, this nook of a kitchen is a shrine to their shining endeavour. Or possibly, given the stippling of food stains everywhere (Barry confesses to being a temperamental cook), more of a grotto.

Fading photographs from early productions by the Kelvinside Young People's Amateur Dramatic Arts Society nestle beside autographed line-ups from appearances in charity galas. The experiences of these years have left Victor and Barry looking remarkably unsullied.

'How old are ...?' Age is something we do not discuss,' admonishes Barry with a smile. 'We feel ageless. But it's no secret that we've been on the go for a number of years.' Peter Pans then? 'Oh yes,' Victor chuckles. 'Only we don't fly, or at least, only off the handle!' They exchange a look of mutual pleasure at this witticism.

They display such resilient style, such outgoing wit, optimism and yet, such dignified reticence over personal disappointments, like childhood. 'Sad, but happy,' says Victor.

As they cheery-bye me down the stairs, I feel I want to give them something in return for their hospitality. Hurriedly I push my own quarter of violet creams into Victor's hand. Sweets for two real sweeties.

MARY BRENNAN

A couple of swells: Victor and Barry

Forbes

We also began our foray into radio when we teamed up with the producer David Jackson-Young from BBC Radio Scotland, and created a spoof documentary entitled *Victor and Barry: That's the Way It Is*. It opens with David calling Vic and Baz at home as he's having trouble finding 22B Lacrosse Terrace in Kelvinside. It becomes clear that the boys have slightly elevated their domain and they actually live just over the border in, er, Maryhill!

David begins: 'Every now and again the tide of showbusiness throws up a couple of extraordinary talents, only to leave them stranded like expiring fish on the shores of the entertainment world. Victor MacIlvaney and Barry McLeish, founder members and musical stalwarts of Kelvinside Young People's Amateur Dramatic Arts Society, are two such talents. MacIlvaney and McLeish are theatrical amateurs in every sense of the word: they love what they do but they're not very good at it. And yet they persist, still convinced that the fame and fortune that has eluded them for so many years will one day be theirs. What keeps people like them going? I visited Victor and Barry to discover more about them, and about the twilight am-dram world they inhabit.'

Alan

That's the Way It Is was the beginning of a long and fruitful relationship with David and BBC Radio Scotland. We soon embarked together on a series of interviews with former protégés of V&B at KYPADAS who had gone on to bigger and better things. The show was called *Scones and Tea with V and B*.

Forbes

I went back to the Tron in the autumn to play Benvolio in Michael Boyd's production of *Doctor Faustus*.

It was a bit of a cursed production. Peter Ling the designer had painted necromantic symbols all over the set. During the dress rehearsal, which was going on well after midnight, someone in the company deliberately set off the fire alarm. After the first night, I got the worst review in my entire career. Mary Brennan in the *Glasgow Herald* wrote, 'Forbes Masson adds little but length to a three-hour production'. Another night, a technician accidentally spilled a pint of beer on the lighting desk and all the lights fused, mid-show.

But this was not to prove to be the only disaster. During the run, one actor got arrested (twice!) and was eventually locked up in Barlinnie. On the last night, his understudy, somewhat bizarrely, got some meat stuck in his throat which had to be surgically removed, and Michael Boyd had to go on in the role.

The Victor and Barry pantomime *Babes in the Wood* was the next show in there, and I was adamant to Peter Ling, who was also designing it, that the necromantic symbols had to be painted over, as I didn't want the panto jinxed. The words of those two men who had been devil hunting at the Harry Younger Hall in 1984 came flooding back to me. 'We must beware!' It took many coats of paint, because the symbols kept shining through. Spooky.

Our *Babes in the Wood* was set in Kelvinside, with Victor and Barry cast as precocious young boys who escape from their nanny and are lured underneath the Kibble Palace in Kelvingrove by Dr Vivien Section. This evil medic was turning people into animals and vice versa. The animals eventually gang together to defeat Vivien Section and they all escape back home.

We had a jolly-hockey-sticks type pantomime boy/collie, played by Hazel Eadie who I had met in Perth's *Peter Pan*, when she played an ostrich); we had Deirdre, the bear from Airdrie; there was a sax-playing Finlay Welsh; Marshall the Chicken was played by the musical director Iain Johnstone who arranged all the songs; and Warren the Rabbit/ Morwenna the Seagull was played by *Game of Thrones/Gangs of London* star, Michelle Fairley. At one point Victor and Barry are transformed into pink and blue poodles and made to dance to the Bay City Rollers as torture. It was all very silly. But fun. It was directed by Hamish Glen.

Alan

Babes in the Wood was a massive hit, but I fear a little bit of the Faustus curse was still lingering. One afternoon playing to a matinee audience of mainly people bussed in from an old folk's home, Victor and Barry had a scene where they spoke directly to the audience, imploring 'What are we going to do?!' One disgruntled ancient audience member retorted, 'Away and work!'

Forbes

Also, during the very last performance, we were pushing the set offstage when it completely fell apart. We came offstage and said, 'It's the first time we've been upstaged by a set.' To which the late, great Sandy Neilson, who had been playing the evil Dr Vivien Section replied, 'No, it's the first time you've been upset by a stage!'

Sandy had not been free from mishaps either. He was an avid crossword enthusiast and had been doing *The Guardian*'s cryptic one in his dressing room between scenes. He made an evil entrance, still wearing his reading glasses. But perhaps the biggest cock-up was when Alan and I were preparing in the dressing room while Sandy performed his opening (and evil) monologue. At the time, Victoria Wood's *Acorn Antiques* was a huge TV hit, and Alan and I knew the 'making of' script inside out. In the dressing room we were reciting Julie Walters' famous lines as Mrs Overall: 'I am a huge, huge star!' Unbeknownst to us, the sound engineer (the same technician who had spilled his pint on the lighting desk in *Doctor Faustus*) brought up the wrong radio mic, so instead of Sandy Neilson's villainous words, the audience got us delivering our Mrs Overall. Oops.

Alan

While performing at the Tron, we got to do some publicity filming on the legendary Glen Michael's *Cartoon Cavalcade* on STV. This was a major TV show for us when we were kids. Glen Michael had been an actor who worked with Rikki Fulton and that ilk, but was now a stalwart on TV with his Sunday afternoon kids cartoon show, featuring Felix the Cat, Spider-Man, Bugs Bunny etc. It was massive in Scotland at the time. I think Glen got a bit scared of our anarchic energy. He looks slightly bewildered in the clip, but it was a bit of a marketing coup being on it.

BABES IN

The Babes in the Wood, alias the precocious Victor and Barry, at the Tron, Glasgow.

Michelle Fairley Remembers...

I remember the rehearsal room for *Babes in the Wood* being so small that when everyone was in, it was chocka block. I played three parts: Warren, an Irish dancing rabbit, the boys' mum, and Morwenna (who I think was a bird, possibly a seagull?). I'd never done anything like it before or since. It seemed like chaos but it was such a laugh. Everyone embraced the surreal madness of the boys' script and threw themselves right into it 100%. Happy days.

Forbes

We were clearly flavour of the year at STV because they asked us to perform live on their New Year show, from the studio in Cowcaddens, alongside a slew of Scottish favourites like Terry Neason, Aly Bain, Jean Redpath, Tam White, Phil Cunningham, Arnold Brown (and why not?), Jungr and Parker, and Peter Nardini. We performed 'A Smile Costs Nothing', a song from *Babes in the Wood*, alongside Jack Docherty and Moray Hunter who were doing their Don and George characters from *Absolutely*, as well as some schtick with Dave Anderson about the obvious error that it was in fact us who were actually meant to be hosting the show.

Alan

It was a hoot, but the thing about performing live on a New Year show is that you don't finish work till around 1.30am, and you are stone cold sober while all your friends and loved ones who have come along to support you in the studio audience are pished! So, it was a tired and binge-drinking-to-catch-up pair who saw in January 1st 1988, a year that was to be even busier for Victor and Barry.

THE WOOD

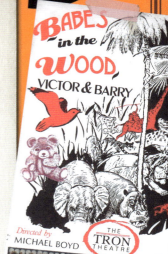

THE COLLIE AND THE CARNOUSTIE QUESTION

- How did we write the panto? Well, we got a piece of paper and pen.
- That's not funny.
- I know, but it used up another ten words.
- Oh good. Seriously though, in May of this year, Michael Boyd asked us to find a well-known panto and adapt it to suit the somewhat limited talents of Victor and Barry (they'd very kindly agreed to star in it without seeing the script beforehand).
- We eventually settled on *Babes in the Wood*, although it wasn't really our first choice. We really wanted to do *Jack and the Beanstalk*, except Barry is afraid of heights, and Victor has a goose phobia.
- They also both felt it was a little height-ist.
- To cut a long story short… what we've gone for is a good old-fashioned adventure story, which I think will excite both children and adults alike. We had a great time working out all the different characters. Apart from Victor and Barry, there's a mad scientist, a principal collie, a magic seagull, a hippy chicken as well as mummy, daddy and a home help. The whole thing is set in that magical, faraway place… Kelvinside, and the tale begins on Christmas Eve.
- It's a very cosmopolitan panto. That's not really due to its content, more to do with the exotic locations in which it was conceived. They include: Falkirk, Glasgow, Shetland, London, the beach in Carnoustie, a chalet in St Andrews (which, incidentally, was totally devoid of light, heat and water), and lots of trains. The last few words were penned during an alcohol-induced haze in a kitchen in, wait for it, Carnoustie.
- Why does Carnoustie feature so prominently in the creation of this epic, you may ask. Well, it's none of your business. The first day of rehearsals was really scary. The whole staff of the Tron… directors, stage managers, designers… and worst of all, actors, all sitting round reading our script for the first time. Normally, the only performers we write for are Victor and Barry, so we're not really used to intelligent, artistic criticism of our work.
- Anyway, there's no going back now. The handouts are printed, the seats are selling fast, we open on December 9th and we'd like to crawl into a little corner and come out in January when it's all over. Never mind how we wrote the panto… *why* did we?

Comics set for fun in forest

COMEDIANS Victor and Barry took to the woods yesterday to research their panto roles.

They did not find any monsters in the undergrowth at Glasgow's Botanic Gardens, but it could be a different story when Babes In The Wood opens at the city's Tron Theatre next Wednesday.

The comics will be busy over Christmas hosting a BBC radio programme, and co-hosting the Hogmanay Show on STV.

Scones and Tea

with David Steel MP

David Steel MP was leader of the Liberal Party for 12 years and integral to its evolution into the Liberal Democrats. He later entered the House of Lords and was also elected a Member of the Scottish Parliament at its inception in 1999. But this all pales into significance alongside his early triumphs with the Kelvinside Young People's Amateur Dramatic Arts Society. His famous 1981 speech 'go back to your constituencies and prepare for government' will be long forgotten before people stop talking about his Peter Pan.

From 1983 he was joint leader of the SDP/Liberal Alliance with David Owen, and the troubled relationship between the 'Two Davids' was of course broached by Victor and Barry for this episode of their BBC Radio Scotland show *Scones and Tea with V and B*. Plus, at the time of their meeting in the Houses of Parliament in 1988, David had recently stood down and was no longer leader of a political party for the first time since 1976. This was also on the boys' agenda. We hear the bells of London's Big Ben ringing in the background as Victor and Barry greet us.

Barry: Hello there, fans!

Victor: Greetings, punters!

B: This week, in our series of in-depth probes into our former members…

V: …of the Kelvinside Young People's Amateur Dramatic Art Society.

B: Yes. We have wound our weary way to Westminster.

V: Oh, I thought we were in Blackpool.

B: No, no, no, that's Big Ben over there.

V: Oh, I see.

B: This is the powerhouse of politics.

V: Yes, and we're here today to meet one of the cogs in the machine.

(We hear some gramophone music and we cut to inside the Houses of Parliament.)

B: Now just speak clearly into the microphone. Tell us your name, and what you had for breakfast.

David Steel: My name is David Steel and I didn't have any breakfast, which is why I'm looking forward to these lovely scones you've been kind enough to bring.

V: Why didn't you have breakfast? Are you on a diet?

D: No, just I never have breakfast. Do I look as though I need to go on a diet?

V: Well, I didn't really want to say anything.

B: Anyway David, tea? What do you take in your tea?

D: Just a little milk please. Milk in first!

B: Oh sorry. You have that one Victor.

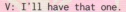

V: I'll have that one.

B: No sugar?

D: No sugar, no.

V: Sweet enough, eh?

D: Sweet enough.

B: There's your milk, there's your tea. That's a lovely yellow tea pot.

D: Very nice, yes.

B: That's really your colour, yellow, isn't it?

D: Yes, the room's...

V: Yellow.

B: Cf course, David, we go back a long way, don't we?

D: Mm-hmm

B: We do. We remember you when you came to audition for us in Kelvinside.

V: When you took the part of Peter Pan, remember that?

D: I do, yes. That was one of my more successful auditions, because I failed some auditions later. But we all have our disappointments.

B: Uh huh.

D: But that was a great success.

V: Peter Pan? Because you met your wife there, didn't you?

D: Yes.

V: She was playing the part of the shadow.

D: Yes, we've sort of had a role reversal ever since.

B: Scone, David? Help yourself to a scone.

D: Oh yes, thank you. That's kind, especially as I had no breakfast.

B: Now of course, the Never Never Land, David; you always wanted to go to the Never Never Land. Is that why you became a Liberal?

D: Well, I think that's a rather unkind way of putting it.

V: He's an unkind man.

D: I don't remember him being quite as sharp as that.

B: Would you like another scone, David?

D: No, I'm still finishing this. Anyway, no it wasn't the Never Never Land. I suppose Peter Pan after all; it's the character that's ever youthful, isn't he?

B: And you certainly are.

D: Well, thank you. I wasn't fishing for that compliment.

V: Do you use moisturizer?

D: No, certainly not.

B: Are your teeth your own, David?

D: Some of them. Yes, some of them.

B: So, you don't rent them then?

D: Oh no, no, no, I don't. They're my own in that sense. They're paid for

B: Oh, went private, did you?

D: Certainly not, no. Don't you know that nowadays, even on the national health, you have to pay? I don't know what the country's coming to.

V: That's the curse. That's the curse.

D: Are your teeth private?

B: Oh no.

V: Barry got his from a catalogue.

B: Yes.

V: Pretty dental theme to this interview.

B: Well, this room is right like a dentist's meeting room, isn't it?

V: I wouldn't say that.

D: This is my new office; I've just moved here. Don't you like it?

V: It's quite cozy.

B: Intimate.

D: Yes.

B: Why have you moved? Because you're not sort of the leader of the... because there isn't one anymore, is there?

D: No, there is a.... yes, of course there is a leader.

B: No, I don't mean a leader, I mean a party.

D: There's a party too, yes.

B: But not the one that you used to be the leader of?

D: Well, it's sort of got bigger; it's joined together, you see.

V: You were always wanting to merge when you were in the company. You wanted

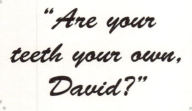

"Are your teeth your own, David?"

us to merge with other companies.

D: Exactly, yes. So, we've been getting bigger, you see, in joining up with others.

V: So, have you retired then?

D: Certainly not. I was just going to say this room is actually nicer than the room I had when I was a grandee.

V: Really?

D: Oh yes.

B: That's showbiz for you, isn't it?

D: I know. It compares well with all the dressing rooms you've been in I should imagine.

B: Talking of dressing rooms, David, we always remember you giving us little pep talks before our shows. Do you remember those?

D: I was always inclined to do that.

B: Saying things like 'go back to your dressing rooms and prepare for the show'. Do you remember?

D: Yeah, I've used that quite a lot.

V: You have, haven't you?

B: To great effect.

D: Oh yes.

B: You're a very good orator.

D: Well, thank you.

B: Tell us… excuse me, I've got a bit of scone on my mouth here. Tell us about your battle bus, David.

D: Oh, that was very theatrical.

V: It was, wasn't it?

D: Yes, I mean that definitely you could say had its origins in the Conserv… in the Kelvinside company.

B: You nearly said 'Conservative' there.

V: That was a wee Freudian slip!

D: Anyway, the bus, well, it was my idea.

B: Was it?

D: Oh yes, way back in 1979. I've had three, you see.

V: Have you?

D: Yeah, three different ones.

V: Did you crash them all?

D: People used to think I owned them, but you don't, you hire them. And actually, it's a very sad story, but the second one, they always were used by pop groups afterwards. And the second one was in that awful crash in Newcastle.

V: Oh dear.

D: What was the name of that group?

B: Bucks Fizz?

D: Yeah, the same bus.

B: What do you think of Bucks Fizz incidentally?

D: I've always made it a rule, never talk about things you don't know anything about. It's quite a good rule in life.

B: David! I'd like to interject here, because I think you know quite a lot about being a recording artist, do you not?

D: A recording artist? Oh, I know what you're getting at.

V: Do you?

D: Yes, my hit.

B: Your hit.

D: Ah yes, well it wasn't a hit really.

B: No.

V: It's been deleted actually, we tried to get a copy. Couldn't get it anywhere, David.

D: Oh well, I mean they're very scarce.

B: They are collectors' items.
D: Very much so.
B: What was it called?

(David starts to laugh)

V: Come on, David.
D: 'I Feel Liberal All Right'. Yes, terrible name.
V: When's the album coming out?
D: Well, we never got beyond the one record.
V: Really?
D: So obviously you can't have an album unless you've got others, I think.
V: But you've always been a bit of an actor though.
D: Well, you have to be, I think. If you go into politics, that's part of it, isn't it? I mean look at…
B: Pretending for all those years that you actually liked Dr Owen.
D: *(slightly choking)* Oh, that was slipped in there!
V: Do you eat an apple a day?
D: No, I don't. I nearly choked on that tea.
B: It's a bit cold, do you want a wee top up?
D: A wee top up. That's lovely, thank you very much.
B: Oh, I should have put your milk in first, you like it that way.
D: No, that's all right. You've put in quite a lot before.
B: So, you've been a recording artist, you've been an author, you've had a battle bus. Now David, you live in the Borders.
D: Yes.
B: That's your constituency.
D: That's right, and my home.
B: Tell us, when you go back home to the Borders (we've seen a lot of photos of you at home in the Borders), do you get fed up of hanging over gates in jumpers, having your photograph taken?
D: It does get a bit repetitive, that's true. The last lot I had were just this very weekend, and do you know what it was?
B: Hanging over a gate with your jumper?
D: Yes, but you don't know which programme it was.
V: Oh, I see, no tell us.
D: No, well, there was no end to my ambitions: it was *The Animals Roadshow*.
B: So, there's another facet of you?
D: Absolutely.
B: You're into animals.

D: Mm-hmm
B: What kind?
D: Dogs. And horses.
V: What sort of dogs do you like?
D: Well, I have a Labrador and a Flat-Coated Retriever.
B: We have a pet seal.
V: Yes, we have.
D: Oh yes?
V: Uh-huh. Our seal is called Shirley Bassey. And we got it so that it would clap at us when we perform in our living room.
D: Because nobody else does, or what?
V: Well, that was a bit cruel.
D: Well, you know, one has to give as good as one gets on these interviews.
V: Well, our tea cups are running dry here.
B: David, the right honorable David Steel MP, your highness...
V: Your worship
B: Thank you so much.
D: It's been a real pleasure to have you here, and to eat your scones.
V: The pleasure has been all yours David.

(More gramophone music and then we cut to outside again and the sound of Big Ben ringing.)

V: Oh, that was exciting.
B: Wasn't it?
V: Small office though.
B: Small man.
V: Big appetite.
B: He walloped through the scones, didn't he?
V: Hmm. Judy can't be feeding him.
B: No. Oh look at that time, we'll miss our bus.
V: Maybe that blonde lady with the blue suit over there will give us a lift (they both gasp in horror). It's her!

(We hear Victor and Barry retching)

The End

1988

SEA SCOUTS
MINI MAHABHARATA
CUT-OUTS CAKE
TONGUE TWISTERS
PERRIER PICKS

Forbes

No sooner had the nippy-heided hangover of STV's *New Year Show* dissipated, both Alan and I headed to Tayside. At Dundee Rep, we would play Phil and Spanky in Alan Lyddiard's production of John Byrne's *Cuttin' a Rug*, the second play of his *Slab Boys Trilogy*. Byrne designed the production while the cast included Vincent Friell, Katy Murphy, Caroline Paterson and Robert Carlyle. Robbie Coltrane, who played Spanky in the original production, came up to Dundee to see it.

The wonderful Scottish actress Irene Sunters played the tea lady, Sadie. One night Irene was a little late making an entrance with her tea trolley, and shouting her opening line of 'Tea's up!'

The cue for her entrance was Alan as Phil saying 'He was in the Sea Scouts'. This particular night, Irene didn't appear as she had slightly missed her cue. A few seconds passed and then her trolley crashed through the door of the slab room followed by a flustered Irene shouting, 'Sea Scouts!'

There was then a slight pause while she realised her mistake and recalibrated, before she said very quietly, 'Tea's up.' It was very difficult to carry on with the scene. Alan, Alec Westwood (who was playing Hector) and I gathered round the tea trolley and were laughing hysterically into our mugs.

Alan

Irene turned 70 during the run of the play, and we all clubbed together to get her a cake made in the shape of the slingback shoes she wore to the office party as Sadie, with 'size 70' written on them.

Soon after *Cuttin' a Rug*, we both worked together again on a new production of *Great Expectations*, a co-production between TAG (Glasgow Citizens Theatre's touring company) and the Gregory Nash Dance Group. The Dickens book was adapted for the stage by Jo Clifford, directed by Ian Brown and choreographed by Nash. The cast was made up of actors as well as contemporary dancers, crossing into each other's territories: so the actors danced and the dancers acted. We did this strange photo shoot for pre-publicity.

JOHN BYRNE'S
CUTTIN' A RUG

Part II of THE SLAB BOYS TRILOGY

Forbes

We both had a tremendous time working on it. It was very atmospheric and hard work, as we threw ourselves into the dancing which gave us very sore feet. Alan played the central role of Pip and I played two roles: Jaggers the lawyer and Mr Wopsle. When I made my entrance as Jaggers, I would walk on to a very loud rhythmical drum beat before I stopped and delivered the line 'My name is Jaggers.' One night I walked on to the drum beat and said, 'My name is Jagger.' A few seconds after realising I had got the crucial name wrong, I added, '...s.' It was difficult for my fellow actors to contain themselves after that. It was a very exciting production and we called it the mini *Mahabharata* (Peter Brook's masterpiece which was playing at the Old Transport Museum at that year's Mayfest, and also immortalised with a mention in Victor and Barry's song 'Glasgow'). We toured the show across Scotland and the north of England to great critical success.

Alan

Victor and Barry opened the entire Mayfest festival with a one-off show at the Theatre Royal. We called it *Victor and Barry Say Goodbye* and was the first of our rather cheeky fake retirement shows. At that point we had no plans to stop doing Victor and Barry, but we enjoyed teasing that they were forever on the point of retirement. The twist this time was that we were saying goodbye to Ophelia Wishart, our wardrobe mistress.

Forbes

I remember the show opened with Alan wandering onstage on his own, looking around for me, slightly annoyed. Then I popped up through a trap door on a piano stool while sipping from a teacup. I then set it on the piano and started to play our anthem 'Kelvinside Men'. I remember being completely blown away by the ferocious laughter and applause from the audience. It felt like we were in a wind tunnel. I don't think Victor and Barry ever got a better or bigger reaction.

The place was packed, and my mum and dad were there. It was such a huge night and I guess the adrenaline got to my head. At one point I was meant to say, in response to a gag, 'Oh that kills me every time.' But what I actually said was 'Oh that

---

AND IT'S GOODBYE FROM THEM

IT pains me to have to say this, but there is no doubt that the Royal Shakespeare Company are exclusively to blame for the untimely demise of Victor and Barry.

Had the two incandescent leading lights of Kelvinside Young People's Amateur Dramatic Society not visited London and bought tickets for the RSC's adaptation of the Stephen King psycho-thriller Carrie, none of it would have happened.

It was this bold and innovative breaking of new ground that inspired Glasgow's most celebrated Thespians to have a crack at this exciting, new theatrical genre. Well, why not?

Gallants

Not for Victor MacIlvaney and Barry McLeish the tunnel vision that afflicts so many other lesser amateur dramatic groups, who cling securely to the tried and tested security of the well-worn classics, no sir.

I mean, for heaven's sake, what kind of shape would amateur theatre be in today if we all timidly refused to dip our toes occasionally into the experimental waters of challenging new art forms?

But I digress. Anyway, fired with enthusiasm, our two gallants returned to Glasgow and immediately plunged KYPADS into a hectic rehearsal schedule for a season of quite brilliant adaptations of some of the classics of horror.

"The first one we tackled," said Barry, "was our version of the Texas Chain Saw Massacre, which we

called the Govan Fish Knives Fiasco."

"Then," chipped in Victor breathlessly, "we had a go at Sweeney Todd, the demon barber of Fleet Street. We entitled it Irvine Ru the Demon Coiffeur of West N Street."

But little did they know that wh they would come to tackle their ol est project to date, an underwate ballet entitled Minnows — their ex citing adaptation of Jaws — traged. was just waiting to strike.

Just when they all thought it was safe to go back in the water, Ophelia Wishart, their renowned wardrobe mistress, dived too deep in the special tank they had designed and built — at enormous expense — for the

piece, suffered a serious attack of the bends and died.

Said Barry: "We cannot imagine KYPADS without her, so, sadly, Victor and Barry must say goodbye to their public, those wonderful audiences who have supported us so faithfully over the years."

It has been my privilege over that time to keep ...

VICTOR AND BARRY: some quite brilliant adaptations.

THEATRE
By MALCOLM REID

Theatre Royal, Glasgow
MARY BRENNAN

Victor and Barry say Goodbye

SO, Victor and Barry have said "Goodbye." A great start to Mayfest that. Kelvinside's bijou thespians threatening to hang up their monogrammed blazers and leave their myriad aficionados pining for the remembered strains of Lower Largo Triangle and other such insouciant ditties.

Don't worry, Glasgow — the truth's miles better. Sensitive to a fault — particularly each other's, but that didn't really *spoil* anything ... temperament can be the spice of laughter — anyway, sensitive to the recent passing of their loyal wardrobe mistress Ophelia Wishart, these rising stars of the Kelvinside am-dram scene gathered together in a farewell memorial spectacular. Songs from some of Kelvinside Young People's Amateur Dramatic Art Society's bravest ventures, anecdotes from behind the scenes of their life together, and yes! anthems for the groomed youth and des res ambience of their beloved Kelvinside — Victor and Barry (abetted, as ever, by the supportive Forbes Masson and Alan Cumming) pulled out all the stops that a West End address allows.

Their idiosyncratic, piquant observation of what constitutes *style*, their flair for presenting a number with just the right degree of Partick pzazz, above all their appetite for adulation, positively delights their families — oops! fans who will be glad to know that their favourite mega-celebrities haven't said Goodbye, merely Au Revoir (and please buy the cassette).

MAYFEST DIARY

GREAT EXPECTATIONS: SEE TUE 10. 'When people think of dance/theatre/music collaborations they expect high-kicking Bonnie Langford-type Great Expecta-a-a-tions! So we have this joke in rehearsals that we're trying to get a high kick somewhere in the play. It hasn't happened yet.'

Nor is it likely to, for TAG Theatre's new adapatation of Dickens' classic, under Ian Brown's direction, is a very un-show biz combination of movement-based dance, atmospheric music and non-caricatured acting. Taking the central role of Pip is Alan Cumming better known as one half of Kelvinside's Victor And Barry. So how do the demands of contemporary dance differ from those of the Young People's Amateur Dramatic Art Society?

'It's certainly changed my social habits,' says Cumming. 'I've stopped drinking and drastically reduc ... bec ... reali ... wor ... she ... tho ... our ... so ...

th ... c ...

and playwright John Clifford in what promises to be a stimulating re-creation of Dickens' world. Even with a script that is continually evolving in rehearsal, it is no mean feat for Clifford to have condensed the broad scope of the novel into play format. 'John has done a cracking job,' says Cumming. 'Some of the ...ptive bits are just ...

the cinema. 'Everyone's being very truthful about it,' explains Cumming. 'The movement helps with that.' What they are working towards is not so much an overstated character comedy as a quirky charm refined by the concentration on movement.

Meanwhile, back in the wonderful world of Am Dram, Alan Cumming is teaming up with Forbes ... acting in ...

fucking kills me every time.' I hadn't realised I had said it until I was told afterwards. I did wonder why there had been a strange shocked hush then raucous laughter after I said the line. A fan made us a piano cake with little cut-out Victors and Barrys. Here we are eating it.

Alan
And here we are with said fan Wilma (wearing her Victor and Barry Are Arty T-shirt) at the Theatre Royal stage door.

I remember that night as being a real turning point. I don't think either of us had realised how much people had taken Victor and Barry to their hearts. We performed a lot of new material which is always terrifying to do, let alone at the Theatre Royal on the opening night of your city's arts festival! But everything worked so well and it honestly felt like we were flying. I knew that people loved us, but that night I felt we had become beloved. It was palpable, and that show was one of the most electrifying experiences I've ever had in the theatre.

Forbes
We closed this special show with a special new song, 'Glasgow', with a backing track arranged by Iain 'Warren the Rabbit' Johnstone. 'Glasgow' was a song born out of the zeitgeist. Glasgow and Scotland were changing and gaining in confidence, as were Victor and Barry. As were Alan and Forbes. Glasgow. An amazing city. A city of immigrants, like a mini New York. The audiences in Glasgow are some of the most honest in the world. If they like you, they love you. It's a very theatrical city, with the world-renowned Citi-

If you are lonely or suffering from a bereavement
We know the place youse really ought to be
A town with guts, you see some on the pavement
High standard of public convenience all for free
It couldn't be better, it sticks out a mile
Although it tends to rain a lot, the people always smile (cos they're guttered!)
We're talking Glasgow, it makes our hearts go funny when we think of it
Just walk along those streets see what we mean – they've been stone cleaned
Go to fig London, we're not like you, we're not capitalists, you're done in
You took a fall, when we've got the Mahabharata at the Transport Hall, just to cap it all
Glasgow (Glasgow)
It's a cultured city and we don't mean penicillin (oh no, oh no)
The people have names like Senga, Shug and Lloyd (Senga, Shug and Lloyd!)
Some of them aren't quite the full shilling (oh no, oh no)
You'd be the same if you were unemployed
There's a plethora of parks, which have thickets full of trees
Chicken korma comes pre-packed, just take it from the freezer for your dinner
It's a winner!
It's Glasgow, it makes our hearts go funny, when we think of it
There's no way you can say that Glasgow's past it, it's been sand blasted
Stuff Auchtermuchty, we proclaim that Glasgow's got what it takes
Just take a shufti, no need to fret, or even hedge your bets, you're on an easy win, if you're Glaswegian
In Glasgow (Glasgow)

Spoken: Glasgow, a city of so many sights,
so many smells, so many drinks, so many cigarettes,
so many heart attacks, so many happy returns to
. . .

Glasgow, it makes our hearts go funny,
when we think of it
Just walk along those streets, see what we mean
They've been stone cleaned
Stuff Auchtermuchty, we proclaim that Glasgow's
got what it takes
Just take a shufti, no need to fret, or even
hedge your bets, you're on an easy win
If you're Glaswegian
In Glasgow (Glasgow)
Glasgow oh oh oh oh oh oh
Gla la la la la, Gla la la la la, Gla la la la la
Glad I live in Glasgow
We belong to Glasgow, dear old Glasgow toon
Glasgow, Glasgow!

zens Theatre and The Tron, and also having that rich heritage from the old music-hall days.

In the old days, the rich lived on the outskirts, while most of Glasgow's populace lived in the city's centre where the energy was very honest, working class and strong. To this day it's a very friendly, sociable city. Glasgow had given us such support, from drama school to the warmth and affection towards Victor and Barry, two Glaswegian characters played by outsiders. We wanted to give some of that affection back.

The song celebrates the city and our love for it, but is also a bit cheeky and Scottish by still being able to point out its bad points: 'A town with guts, you see some on the pavement / So many drinks, so many cigarettes, so many heart attacks'. In the '80s there was an ad campaign to boost the city called Glasgow's Miles Better, with Mr Happy from the *Mr Men* books as the logo. In 1988 Glasgow hosted the Garden Festival and a huge swathe of the Clyde riverside was being redeveloped as part of this rejuvenation. Glasgow was clearly becoming the place to be. And we were proud to be part of it. During Mayfest we were interviewed by the legendary Tony Wilson as part of STV's coverage. We filmed a video for our song 'Glasgow', with Victor and Barry dancing in various Glasgow locations.

Alan

Victor and Barry were back on Scottish TV screens on May 29th when we co-hosted the Scottish segments of ITV's telethon from the Glasgow Garden Festival with Paul Coia. This involved us staying up all night and greeting members of the public who got progressively more drunk and proffered larger and larger cheques as the night went on. We sang songs and generally mucked about like a sort of Kelvinside Ant and Dec, as well as hosting a talent competition called *Victor and Barry's Search for a Star* where people competed to do the most wacky yet entertaining things. For example, the first contestant sang with his head inside a washing machine. You get the gist. Another sang the Patsy Cline hit 'I Fall to Pieces', which kind of summed up how the programme was going.

This was our first time doing live television. The first time we had earpieces in with the control room shouting instructions to us about wrapping up an interview so we could go to commercial; or telling us we would have to busk (live on air) for a few minutes until the next guest was ready. As dawn broke and our marathon concluded, we had a couple of drinks and some prawn cocktails but then had to go back live on air, a bit pished. It was a very, very surreal experience, but we loved it.

Comedy duo Victor and Barry

Alan Cumming

Forbes

We continued touring with *Great Expectations*, then Alan went off to the Traverse to work on a new play, *Conquest of the South Pole*. And I went back to the Tron.

That year, Michael Boyd made a further journey into the world of old Glasgow music hall and variety traditions, by reviving the Five Past Eight shows. These had been massive in the '40s, '50s and '60s in the old Alhambra Theatre, and had launched the careers of Stanley Baxter, Rikki Fulton and Jack Milroy. Michael's take was to bring some of those old stars back alongside more current acts. He asked me to do some stand-up. On my own. At first, I was afraid, I was petrified, I felt I could not perform without Alan by my side; but after the initial terror it proved to be a tremendous experience.

I came up with a surreal nerdy character called Rodney the Sex Machine. He turned out to be very popular. One night's performance also had Jack Milroy and his wife Mary Lee on the bill. They were hysterically funny. I talked to them before the show, telling Jack how much I had enjoyed his performances over the years, and the debt Victor and Barry owed to Francie and Josie. He said he was so pleased that Victor and Barry had been complimentary about them on STV's *Review of the Year* in 1987.

On the strength of my stand-up success, Michael asked me to headline a Christmas show and I was also invited onto a new Channel 4 arts programme from Glasgow called *Halfway to Paradise*. I eventually took Rodney to the Gilded Balloon for the 1990 Edinburgh Fringe. I had been growing in confidence with the solo stand-up, but one afternoon at the Gilded Balloon I was on a bill with magician Fay Presto. The audience for the afternoon's show was very small. I went out, did my act but died a death. I came offstage, white as a sheet. Fay asked me what was wrong. I said 'I died'. She replied, in her posh English theatrical accent, 'Darling, you can never die when there aren't enough people in the audience to bury you.' A mantra I adhere to, even to this day!

Alan

After the success of our run in the Edinburgh Suite at the Assembly Rooms in 1987, Bill Burdett-Coutts asked us back this year for a longer run and in a bigger venue: The Ballroom. We got new publicity shots done…

However, it still felt strange being the 'local' act, and as we said in our 'Edinburgh Festival Song', 'the place is like an Oxbridge Ghetto'. It seems strange to say it now, considering the great success we were having, but we both still felt a little second class in that late '80s stand-up environment. After a performance in the Assembly Rooms bar, Forbes was approached by Vivienne Clore, who was then an agent with The Richard Stone Partnership in London, and represented Victoria Wood, who we idolised. She said she loved Victor and Barry, gave Forbes her card and said she was interested in representing us. We talked it over and then met with her and Meg Poole (the drama agent in that agency), and decided to sign up. Vivienne (or Clorissa, as Victor and Barry were to come to call her) and Meg were instrumental in helping us move on to the next stage of both our Victor and Barry and Forbes and Alan stages of our careers.

I think of that festival of '88 being a real turning point. Victor and Barry were the hit of the festival comedy world, and *Conquest of the South Pole* was the hot ticket at the Traverse, eventually transferring to the Royal Court in London and earning me my first Olivier Award nomination. At the time, though, it was a logistical nightmare, trying to get from one venue to another in time for the next show. I remember

one time pulling up at the Traverse, having raced across town in a car from the Assembly Rooms and opening the door to get out only to see a cyclist promptly bang into it and somersault over the door onto the pavement in the Grassmarket. Luckily, he got up and said he wasn't badly injured, but it kind of encapsulated the madness of that time for me. Many years later I was in a bar in New York City when a man came up to and said, 'Do you remember a guy on a bike tumbling over your car door at the Edinburgh Fringe years ago?'

'Of course,' I said, wondering where this was going.

'It was me!' he replied gleefully. I bought him a drink, so happy to see him unharmed and alive after all those years of wondering if I had caused irreparable damage.

Forbes

Our Fringe run sold out and we were touted for the prestigious Perrier Award. We didn't win. Jeremy Hardy did. However, Nica Burns (who directed the awards and at the time was Fascinating Aida's manager) was so taken with V and B that she got us on the bill for the Perrier Pick of the Fringe season

Forbes Masson are *Alan Cumming*
Victor and Barry

later that year at the newly reopened Donmar Theatre in London, as well as helping to arrange for us to do a tour of Australia in 1989. Also, the legendary TV writer and producer John Lloyd (*Not the Nine O'Clock News*, *Spitting Image*, *Blackadder*) made a Channel 4 documentary covering 24 hours at the Edinburgh Fringe that year called *39,000 Steps*, and Victor and Barry were his nirvana in a sea of fringe dirge. The show opened with us singing our spoof of the Proclaimers song 'Throw the R Away...'

In the summer, Scottish Opera's music director John Mauceri (who we had met when we did an ad campaign for them) got in touch to ask if I would take part in a concert version of the Kurt Weill musical *Lady in the Dark*, for the Edinburgh International Festival in August. My guess is that I was offered the part because in the movie version the character was played by Danny Kaye who also had red hair. They sent me the score and libretto. The musical is about a woman who's having a breakdown, and in a fantasy sequence she meets a Circus Ringmaster who sings

a patter song about Russian composers. Here is the first verse. It gives you the gist...

RINGMASTER
There's Maliszewski, Rubinstein, Arensky, and Tchaikovsky
Sapellnikoff, Dmitriev, Tcherepnin, Kryzhanovsky
Godowsky, Artsybushev, Moniuszko, Akimenko
Soloviev, Prokofiev, Tiomkin, Koreshchenko

It's an absolutely crazy tongue twister and carries on like this with more complicated Russian names while the music gets faster and faster. I had a look over the music at home and saw that we were rehearsing the following week. I didn't think to learn it as I thought we would do that in rehearsals, like we would with a play. I had never worked with an opera company before and I was about to find out how wrong I was. I walked into the rehearsal room to find a full chorus and orchestra, as well as my fellow actors, Patricia Hodge and

PROCLAIMERS SONG:

We've had enough of being told that our dialect's guff
We're being ostracised cos we stroke our T's and dot our I's
It's not very fashionable being smart, but we don't care for fashion, we live for our art
Some people think our accent has had its day cos we elongate our vowels and throw the 'ch' away

We're sorry if you're not pleased, if you can't translate Kelvinsidese
We know we sound Anglophied, but we're Caledonians inside
What do we need an interpreter for? Their complaints just make us go grr (GRR!)
South of the border, they think that we're freaky

Cos we're as Scottish as a tin of Baxters cock-a-leekie
Yes, we're as Scottish as a tin of Baxters cock-a-leekie

A, E, I, O, youse better believe it
If this carries on, all of these accents will be gone
And they'll be Kelvinside no more, Hyndland no more
Milngavie no more, Bearsden no more
We're talking Kelvinside no more, Hyndland no more
Milngavie no more, Bearsden no more, oh!
It's not very fashionable being smart, but we don't care for fashion, we live for our art
Some people think our accent has had its day
Cos we elongate our vowels and throw the 'ch' away

Victor And Barry

Assembly Rooms

Fringe comedy is dominated by down-beat self-deprecators, rant-mode agit-proppers and right-on rebel-rousers. Someone some-where must have forgotten to tell Victor and Barry. With their brilliantined hair, monogrammed blazers, cravats, and Oxford bags –

they are comic curios, and all the more delightful for that. As they gently bicker and banter they of-fer the audience a stage-door en-try into the dotty world of ama-teur theatre, which they, as founder members of the Kelvinside Young People's Ama-teur Dramatic Arts Society, are in a unique position to do. Follow-ing the lead of the RSC's Carrie, they double-talk their way through the problems of staging a repertory season of horror musi-cals, starting perhaps with Jaws. 'We thought we'd set it a little closer to home,' says Barry, in his trendy thespian smarmy Glaswe-gian drawl. '. . . on the River Kel-vin. And call it Trout.' At regular intervals they burst into song: Marks And Spencers Shopping Adventures, a kind of musical ver-sion of the 60 second shopping spree in which they cram as many items as can be bought there into each verse: a bitter-sweet song in the Kitchen Of Life: and best of all, Glasgow ('a town with guts, you can see them on the pave-ment') proving itself miles better

than London: 'you took a fall when we got the Mahabarata at the Transport Hall'. The last roused the partisan crowd to cheers, albeit in Edinburgh, 'a part of Scotland that remains for-ever English'. Deliciously hammy, hopelessly pun-filled, they con-trived to put the following lines to the climax of Somewhere Over The Rainbow. 'If Robbie Coltrane can get a job at the BBC, then why. . . . oh why, can't we?' It's a good question. *Assembly Rooms (Venue 3), 54 George Street (031-226 2427/8), Mon-Sun until 3 Sept, 5.45-6.55pm* Tristan Davies

---

...EVISION TODAY, September 8, 1988

EDINBURGH FRINGE

Devilish: ALAN CUMMING and FORBES MASSON as Victor and Barry.

Victor and Barry Say Goodbye

BUT NOT for long, we trust, because these two giants of Glasgow artistic and cafe society are too good to let go, even if the young actors who play them, Alan Cumming and Forbes Masson, have thriving careers of their own.

Indeed, the West End is promised a brief glimpse of them later this month, presenting a routine that has charmed and convulsed both Edinburgh and Glasgow theatregoers for a few years now.

Victor Aloysius McIlvaney and Barry Primrose ("but don't you dare mention it") McLeish are, however, firmly rooted in Kelvinside, the hub of Glasgow's artistic endeavour, where they have formed their

It seems to me that, although they come under the heading of "new cabaret", they are presenting a form of character comedy that has been done in Scottish variety theatres for many years, putting me in mind of the youthful Rikki Fulton and Jimmy Logan of 30 years ago, debunking the pretensions of those who live in the "posh" Glasgow suburbs of Bearsden and Milngavie.

own dramatic and musical comedy society, having become dissatisfied with the rough theatre of Partick. Speaking with exquisite precision, with only the occasional "youse" showing their humble origins, they bicker with each other in the manner of Hinge and Bracket, recalling their past triumphs and anticipating future successes.

Their show is a devilish assault on all the "precious" aspects of the show business fan, as well as on the artistic mores of their native city, beautifully timed and presented, and embellished with songs of their own devising, which cleverly remind one of other numbers in a variety of genres.

Marvellously camp without being overtly gay, Victor and Barry deserve to be catego-rised as national treasures. Above all, they prove that it is possible for young performers to be hilariously funny without using one four-letter work or sexual reference.

Peter Hepple

Victor and Barry's cabaret coach tips

Victor MacIlvaney and Barry McLeish, founder members of the Kelvinside Young People's Amateur Dramatic Arts Society, are at this very moment winging their way to the Assembly Rooms, where they will present their wee concert on a nightly basis during the Festival. They are on board a Glasgow to Edinburgh CityLink bus, in seats S15 and S16 (non smoking), where they are sharing a flask of herbal tea, and a quarter pound of chocolates...

'You know, Barry, I'll never forget my first Festival.

Really Victor? Why?

Erm... I've forgotten.

Oh!

Have you been nibbling my Thorntons' Continentals?

No, I have just had my teeth scaled.

Funny you should mention the Ed-inburgh Festival.

Is it?

Not very. But we are in it this year.

Are we? Oh good I like the Edin-burgh Festival, it's sort of like an English version of Glasgow's Mayfest.

Yes I know what you mean. It is a colostomy of culture.

An enema of entertainment.

Anathema of art.

Quite.

Pity about the venues though.

Absolutely. Remember the mime version of Jonathan Livingston Seagull in a toilet?

I couldn't hear a thing for the cis-tern.

And as for the hygiene...

Non-existent.

And the queues?

Talk about the Onedin line...ha ha.

I don't get that, Barry.

All. . . needing . . . line.

Yes?

Queues. For the toilet.

Oh! I see. Ha ha ha.

Ha ha ha.

Ha ha ha ha.

Get a grip, Victor.

And what about the litter.

All those discarded leaflets for shows that no one goes to see.

Apparently they are going to be collected this year and made into a surrealistic sculpture of Mal-colm Rifkind.

Really?

Uh-huh. Then it will be set alight as the show piece of the Festival fireworks display.

That's creativity for you.

But that's the Festival all over, Barry. Creative, innovative, wacky, zany, postgraduate and in-credibly overpriced.

No, Victor, that's the Fringe. The Official Festival is just overpriced.

Mmm.

They do a nice brochure, no?

Oh yes.

Easy to read, colour co-ordinated and fits snugly into most leading brands of personal organisers.

Great.

Of course being part of the Fringe is wonderful.

Meeting Brian Matthews was my personal highlight last year.

He sounds a lot fatter on the radio.

But we do have rather a large wireless.

True.

But it does have its drawbacks. Those digs we were in last year left a lot to be desired.

Extortionate rent, and having to share the kitchen with those Aus-tralian jugglers was a culinary nightmare.

Their recipe for pavlova was a piece of performance art in itself. And then there is the flat in Kelvinside lying empty for three weeks. It's so difficult to find a de-cent geranium-sitter.

Last year, Viola Tuck from next door ruined your sterling work in cross-pollinating your bonsais, Barry.

Victor MacIlvaney and Barry McLeish, Glasgow's answer to ...ard, Say Goodbye at the Assembly Rooms (031-226 2427/8) ...

Don't remind me, Victor, travesty. But you can't in love with them.

What, bonsais?

No, Edinburgh Festival. I'm sorry, I am feeli... coachsick.

The crowded streets, the... the costumes, the se... make-up, the props...

Stop singing, Barry. looking!

Who cares? It's Festiva... hang the dentist's bill, e... other vanilla truffle.

● *Victor and Barry are at th... sembly Rooms from 13 t... Sept, 5.45pm. 031-226 242...*

Richard Griffiths, all off the book, singing away.

My song slowly approached and I got sweatier and sweatier. The intro started and I stuttered my way through the opening of the song. John Mauceri stopped the orchestra, and looked over at me slightly furiously. I had upset someone who had worked with Leonard Bernstein! The opera chorus and musicians tutted and sniggered at my ineptitude. I was whisked off to a small room with a pianist to note bash the song. Fortunately, I am a quick study, and probably because I was used to singing all those Victor and Barry patter songs, I quickly cracked it, went back in the room and delivered! Phew. On the night in the Usher Hall, Alan came and sat in the star-studded audience. The performance was being broadcast live on Radio 2. No pressure. It was scary, but it went extremely well and I loved working with Patricia and Richard (who would soon become a Victor and Barry fan).

After Edinburgh, we took Victor and Barry on a small tour, to Cumbernauld Theatre and the Macrobert Arts Centre at Stirling University. We also did a gig at St Andrews University Students Union, and for the first time in Victor and Barry's career, they died. There were enough people in the audience to bury us, so we made a hasty retreat.

We both started travelling a lot to London for interviews and work. In those days you could just rock up to Glasgow Airport at any time, go through security, walk up to the gate, and wait and see if there were any spare seats on a flight. Then you'd just buy a standby ticket for about £30 and jump on. One day we turned up to see Ross King waiting, talking into what looked like a giant plastic brick with an arial coming out of it. Ross is now huge in LA, reporting on celebrities for TV, but at that time he was a DJ on Radio Clyde, and like us was travelling up and down to London for work opportunities. The giant plastic brick was, of course, one of the first mobile phones. We had never seen one up close before. We thought he was incredibly cool and successful for having one.

Alan

We were invited by BBC radio producer Clive Brill to host *The Word Made Fresh*, a cabaret to launch Radio 4's Young Playwrights Festival. On the bill were poets Lemn Sissay and Benjamin Zephaniah, comedians Miles and Milner, and a very young Steve Coogan. We recorded it in the Paris Studios, where all the old BBC radio comedies I had listened to as a kid were made.

Another radio producer, our BBC Radio Scotland chum David Jackson Young with whom we had recorded the spoof documentary *That's the Way it Is* in 1987, asked us to do a series of celebrity interviews called *Scones and Tea with V and B*. They cemented the conceit of real people pretending to have been former members of the Kelvinside Young People's Amateur Dramatic Arts Society. Our first victim was the MP, and great sport, David Steel.

Victor and Barry going south for the first time to perform at the Donmar Warehouse at the Perrier Pick of the Fringe season was a big deal. But not just in a celebratory, well-done boys, gaun yersels kind of way. There seemed to be concern that we might be too Scottish and that our humour wouldn't travel; another example of that defeatism and self-censorship that we had experienced so many times in our brief careers thus far.

From Kelvinside: Victor and Barry (alias Forbes Masson and Alan Cumming)

Michelle Smith

Legends in their own brunch time

Studio 3: Scones and Tea with V and B Monday 12.47pm (repeated Tuesday 9.15pm) Radio Scotland

VICTOR MCILVANNEY and Barry McLeish are very, mega famous. The reason for this almost legendary stardom is, of course, their position as founder members of the Kelvinside Young People's Amateur Dramatic Art Society, which is the foremost amateur musical society in the whole of Scotland, (not Glasgow.

For the uninitiated, the philistines, the fat people, who may be reading this: Kelvinside is a posh district in Glasgow, a major city in Scotland, which is to the north of England and to the left of Neil Kinnock.

We now eavesdrop on Victor and Barry, as they take a light lunch in their local brasserie ...

Victor: Another portion of *tagliatelle ecossais*, Barry?
Barry: Are you kidding, Victor? I'm stuffed!
V: Oh.

B: Victor, stop dunking your chocolate croissant in your capuccino, people are looking.
V: Sorry, Barry. Oh, rats – a bit's just dropped off!
B: Look at this headline in the paper Victor: the BBC are to be deregulated.
V: Deregulated? What's that?
B: It's a sort of privatisation, Victor. Remember, they did it to the buses.
V: Oh no! That's terrible ... Does that mean that we'll have to wait hours for a programme, and then a lot of them will come on at the same time?
B: Yes, and none of them will be going our way.
V: Just like life, really ... Bung me another slice of that carrot cake, Baz.
B: Now Vic, a moment on the lips ... a lifetime on the hips.
V: Oh.
B: That reminds me, the man from the BBC phoned today. Apparently, before the Beeb gets bought up by Guinness, they want to make a mega series as a last attempt to bring culture to the masses.
V: Whom do they want to appear in it?
B: Us, of course, Victor. After all, we are Britain's major

patronisers of the arts.
V: Mmm.
B: And because we're amateurs, down to earth and not in the least pretentious.
V: *Mais oui.*
B: *Comme d'habitude.*
V: So what will the programmes consist of then?
B: Well, it's going to be us, and a lot of other famous people.
V: Not as famous as us though?
B: No, but the funny thing is, that all these other people started off their careers with us at the Kelvinside Young People's Amateur Dramatic Art Society.
V: Oh yes. The number of talented people we've had working under us.
B: We taught them everything we know.
V: It didn't take long.
B: And all these people, our protegees, want to interview us, so we can impart our wisdom to the nation.
V: So, it'll be a sort of *Wogan* with wit.
B: Yes, and real hair.
V: Sounds exciting.
B: Yes. Hang the waistline: pass the demerara, Victor, I fancy another cocoa.

FORBES MASSON, ALAN CUMMING

Alan Thomson

STV were interested in making a documentary about our odyssey and the seemingly insurmountable challenges we would face trying to crack the London market. We decided to call it *Victor and Barry Take the High Road*. The programme featured Victor and Barry clowning around (the boys trying to communicate with Cockney newspaper vendors was a highlight) and being, as ever, slightly disappointed with their surroundings.

Forbes

Luckily that wasn't too difficult to achieve because, while doing the Donmar shows, we stayed in a freezing little flat in Stoke Newington that belonged to the set designer of *Conquest of the South Pole*, which Alan was soon to do again at the Royal Court Theatre. I remember London being very bleak at the time. Stoke Newington was full of empty shops and dilapidated properties, far from the gentrified upmarket place it is now. One night, there was a riot outside and a car was set on fire. Alan and I had to share a bed, a bit like Laurel and Hardy, though we were both in sleeping bags. I got terrible flu and I seem to recollect me keeping Alan awake with my sweatiness, snoring and coughing.

Alan

Oh, I actually remember constantly wheezing and using my inhaler as the flat was mid-renovation and so incredibly dusty and also rather damp: the perfect combo for an asthmatic. We also discovered we were sharing the flat with a German girl named Tala, but undeterred about this addition to our living arrangements, we decided to write a part for her in the show.

She became Heidi, our au pair.

We actually had a great time writing it and filming in London. In a way this was how we worked best: improvising on the go around a loose structure. We brought in Hazel Eadie, who had been so memorable in *Babes in the Wood* at the Tron. She played a glamorous actress that Victor falls for and drinks champagne from her shoe whilst on a date.

Forbes

We filmed the opening night of the Donmar Warehouse shows. It was really well received. They got it! They understood us! They laughed! They cheered! Richard Griffiths, who I had met during *Lady in the Dark*, was part of the audience and full of praise. He got it too!

SATURDAY Leisure
KELVINSIDE DUO TO HEAD SOUTH

I DON'T know how Terry Wogan might feel about meeting Kelvinside's most famous sons, Victor and Barry, but I can tell you that Vic and Baz are all of a qui

Alan

What had we been worrying about? Well, actually, we had been listening to the voices all around us that we had heard growing up, saying we would have to change and adapt if we wanted to succeed outside of Scotland. This brief run in London made us realise we were right to be our own idiosyncratic selves; that was what made us special, not trying to be generic or anglified.

Meanwhile, Jammy Records in Glasgow had asked us to make an album and we went to the Radio Clyde studios to record it. It was called *Hear Victor and Barry and Faint* and was due for release just in time for the Christmas market.

They made a promo vinyl EP for radio stations to play, which included our Proclaimers parody and the classic Victor and Barry nostalgia-fest 'Why Isn't Things the Way They Used to Be'. The full album was released on state-of-the-art ferric audio cassette.

We had the album launch just in time for Christmas, back in Glasgow at Miss Cranston's Tearooms. I was performing at the Royal Court and flew up for the day. Maybe it was something to do with being so immersed in performing *Conquest of the South Pole* and being away from Scotland for a couple of weeks, but I had somehow forgotten the Victor and Barry frenzy we had engendered at that time. Walking into Miss Cranston's and seeing all the press and TV news crews was quite a shock to me. I remember us being the 'and finally' segment of the news bulletins that night and felt a bit scared. Victor and Barry were taking over! I thought it wasn't right that we should be on the news. Although we continued to perform on and off for a few more

years, and kept writing other projects together, I look back at that album press conference as the moment I started to pull away from Vic and Baz.

Forbes

I did a few shows at the Tron Christmas Present. Alongside Rodney, I created another character called Forties Manhattan, a strange demented Christmas crooner. I came up with the name when I was scouring the press for reviews of *Lady in the Dark*, and one said 'the production evokes Forties Manhattan'. I misread it as 'Forbes Masson'.

Alan and I recorded a special Christmas message for Tron audiences to be screened while we were away in Australia.

STV had asked us to do the *New Year Show* again, but we were going to be out of the country as our flight for Australia left on December 26th. So instead, we shot another version of our Glasgow song, this time with a bigger budget and including a very big finish with a helicopter shot that started with us dancing to the last chorus and pulled out to reveal we were on the top of the Finnieston Crane! Then it kept going and going until the whole of the dear green place was revealed and we were little dots on the horizon.

To achieve this coup de television we had to climb up very small, very high ladders to get to the top of the crane in full costume and wait for the helicopter. It was very windy already and when it arrived we could barely hear the playback from the tiny, tinny speaker hidden at our feet (this was in the days when the only drones available were the noises made by bagpipes). We

didn't have any harnesses or safety equipment. I doubt if health and safety would allow us to do it now, but it does look amazing. And it's incredible to see beneath us not the groovy café society of today's Finnieston and Riverside, but just scrubby wasteland. It's amazing to see how much has changed, and how old it makes us feel!

Alan

We recorded an insert to be played just before the Glasgow video was shown, as if it were a live link from Australia, which we filmed in The People's Palace on Glasgow Green. Nicky Campbell, who was hosting, pretended to talk to us.

We packed our bags, met with our agent Vivienne and jumped on the plane for the long flight to Sydney. Midway through the first leg to Bangkok, the stewardess came towards us with a bottle of champagne and some cake from a mysterious benefactor. The Irish comedian Dave Allen, who Vivienne also represented at the time, had kindly sent the gifts to wish us well Down Under. Our flight was showbiz central as we discovered Cliff Richard was on it too, though not, like us, in economy!

Forbes

Arriving in Sydney, we were driven to the beautiful Elizabeth Bay area where we had been given an apartment each. Vivienne was going to stay with us for the first few weeks to settle us in and get the show on. And then we would be on our own for the rest of the tour which would eventually take us to Adelaide, Alice Springs, Cairns and a little place called Rockhampton. However, we were to open the show at the Sydney Opera House as part of that year's Festival of Sydney! We had about a week to acclimatise, get over the jet lag and also think about script changes to tailor the show for an Australian audience.

They gave us an amazing room to work in at the Opera House with a grand piano and a huge window that overlooked the ocean; there we practiced our songs and worked on rewrites. We discovered that the wannabe upmarket, pretentious area of Sydney (the equivalent of Kelvinside) was Vaucluse. We wrote a special song about coming to Australia with references to *Neighbours*, Kylie and *Prisoner: Cell Block H*. We swam in the Boy Charlton outdoor pool in Woolloomooloo Bay next to the Opera House, discovered Australia's passion for smearing ketchup on top of a pie, and let our skin get used to the intense sunshine.

And, as if it was meant to be, we discovered a brand of beer called VB beer!

On Hogmanay, Vivienne went to bed early as she was tired. Alan and I were at a loose end and feeling very homesick, so went out for a wander and ended up bringing in the New Year sitting on the steps of the Opera House with a couple of cans of VB beer. In the distance we could see a massive marquee with lights and music. It seemed as though people were having a fabulous party. Soon we would find out who those people were.

David Jackson Young Remembers...

It was the mid-1980s and I was working for BBC Radio in Edinburgh when I first got wind of Victor and Barry. The news blew in from the west, specifically from Glasgow. Even more specifically, from Kelvinside. More specifically still, from North Kelvinside. Or Maryhill, as everyone but Victor and Barry themselves would call it.

Had I heard about this up-and-coming double act, asked a colleague one day, two guys in cravates with a piano. 'What: they just wear cravates?' I said. Was this Glasgow's answer to the Chippendales?

But the more I learned about the boys and their cult status as evangelical ambassadors for musical theatre at its most genuinely amateur, the more intrigued I became. I had already made several fly-on-the-wall documentaries about various iconic figures on the Scottish arts scene such as Kenneth McKellar and Larry Marshall.

What if Victor MacIlvaney and Barry McLeish were icons in the making? Wouldn't they be ideal subjects for a similar kind of programme? After extensive and pointlessly protracted negotiations (it might have been quicker if they'd had an agent) they both agreed to take part.

To make a successful fly-on-the-wall documentary, you have to get to know your subjects well. It takes time to form the necessary bonds of trust; for the inhibitions and self-consciousness to melt away; for the façades to drop, and the truth (or truths) to emerge. That's why I spent the best part of an afternoon with MacIlvaney and McLeish, following them from room to room round their North Kelvinside apartment with my tape recorder.

The result was *Victor and Barry: That's the Way it Is*. The title, I think, says it all. When I hear the programme now, almost four decades later, I'm struck by how the boys' initial wariness and suspicion soon give way to warmth and openness. Within minutes of my arrival, they're showing me round their cramped walk-in wardrobe, cheerfully inviting me to fondle their trademark silk dressing gowns, their 'V' and 'B'-embossed blazers. And yes, those famous cravates!

Over scones and tea in the kitchenette, they described the origins of the Kelvinside Young People's Amateur Dramatic Art Society, gossiping playfully about later-to-be-famous members such as Viv Lumsden and Kirsty Wark, and about the Society's great leading lady Renee Roberts, a star whose magic spark, they reminisce fondly, 'brought light to all her parts'.

And when I talk to each of them individually, when for some reason the other one has had to leave the room, they speak with astounding frankness about their personal ambitions. Neither, it emerges, is truly passionate about musical theatre.

'My dream,' says Victor, his voice hushed and a little hoarse, 'is to own a trout farm.'

'My burning ambition,' confides Barry with ill-concealed yearning, 'my *raison d'être*, is to be a fishmonger.'

Every great documentary has its bombshell moment. This was ours. Whether they ever revealed these private passions to each other, I can't say. I suppose that if they heard the programme they must have found out. But then I recall what Victor once said about hating the sound of his own voice, and Barry's swift rejoinder of 'Well, join the club!' Maybe they never could quite bring themselves to tune in.

Perhaps it was these suppressed piscine aspirations that diluted the single-minded ruthlessness so necessary for major success in the entertainment world. I honestly just don't know. At any rate, I never heard from them again.

Victor and Barry: That's the Way it Is was among the highlights of the 1987 Christmas radio schedules. It made Pick of the Month in the Sunday Post. But for me it was time to move on. After 40-odd years in the salmon-smoking business, I've lost touch with the glamorous world of broadcasting and the arts. But a recent STV programme caught my eye: *Maryhill's Got Talent*. If Victor and Barry were still around and still performing, surely they'd be featuring in such a show?

I turned it on with keen anticipation. But it wasn't a musical spectacular. It was a fly-on-the-wall documentary about a six-year-old accordionist and tap dancer from Peebles called Mary Hill. There had been a minor typo in the programme billing.

And yet somehow, wherever they are, whatever they're doing, I feel sure those old-school showbiz stalwarts Victor and Barry would be proud of her.

Scones and Tea

with *Kirsty Wark*

Mirroring her days at the Kelvinside Young People's Amateur Dramatic Art Society when she left a backstage role to take centre stage at the WRI Hall, Kirsty Wark stepped from behind the camera at BBC Scotland and onto our screens. Life has never been the same again. Victor and Barry reunited with Kirsty in her bijou West End apartment for this 1988 episode of their BBC Radio Scotland series *Scones and Tea with V and B*.

At the time, she had yet to assume the mantle of *Newsnight* host, but was doing double duty by fronting both the BBC Scotland political programme *Left, Right and Centre* and co-hosting the network's *Breakfast Time*. Because of her early morning schedule, Kirsty asked to be interviewed by Victor and Barry in her bed. Ever intrepid, they agreed.

Victor: That was lucky the door was on the latch.

Barry: It was, wasn't it?

V: So, here we are in the house.

B: Hope she doesn't mind us snooping in like this. Bit on the untidy side.

V: She doesn't have a lot of time, she's a very busy woman.

B: And because she works in the BBC, she can't be earning a lot.

V: She won't be able to afford a cleaner, will she?

B: No, no. I think this must be the bedroom over here. You know we're meeting her in her bedroom?

V: Never!

B: Yeah.

V: This door here?

B: This is it. She's so busy it's the only place she could see us.

(They knock on the door)

V&B: Hello?

(They open the bedroom door and step inside)

B: Oh, lovely.

V: Oh, very spacious.

(We hear an old gramophone record play)

B: Right, now, take the microphone. Tell us who you are, what you had and who you interviewed for breakfast.

Kirsty Wark: My name is Kirsty Wark and I work for the BBC. I work in Scotland for a political programme called *Left, Right and Centre*, and I also travel down to London to do *Breakfast Time*.

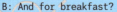

B: And for breakfast?

K: For breakfast, usually a very stale croissant that one of the guests has left half-eaten after the programme.

B: Anyway, Kirsty, enough of dribble-drabble. Would you like some tea, Kirst? May I call you Kirst?

K: Call me Kirst.

V: OK.

K: I usually take chamomile at this time of night, but…

B: Oh, I'm sorry, we're out of medicine. Tea, Kirsty?

K: Tea, please. Could you put the milk in first?

B: Oh, that's not yours. The milk in first? Fussy. Right, here we are.

V: Oh, you spilt it on the duvet.

B: Oh dear, sorry!

K: It doesn't matter, it's a funny colour anyway.

B: Your futon's lovely, if I may say so, Kirsty. A bit uncomfortable for three of us here and David, of course, the engineer.

V: Anyway, Kirst, scone?

K: A bit bad for my digestion at this time of night.

V: Never mind.

K: Don't put crumbs in the duvet, please.

B: No, there's nothing worse in the morning, is there?

V: Itchy, itchy, itchy

K: Nothing worse.

B: Right in your jim-jams with a couple of bits of crumbs. Not a lot of people at home will know this, but many, many years ago when you were young, you started off with us as a prompter, do you remember that?

K: I try to forget it.

B: Well, there was one occasion we were mounting a show called *Oh Liver*. You remember that, Victor?

V: I remember very well because I had a rather un-fortunate foot complaint.

B: Oh yes, it was terrible.

V: Which made me have to withdraw from the part of Mr Sowerberry, the undertaker.

Kirsty: Yes. Well, I remember this…

V: Who stepped in? Who stepped in?

K: Moi!

B: Who took off her hat, took off her glasses, unrolled her hair… you did Kirst, didn't you?

K: It seems so long ago. I had always wanted to play that part.

V: Very masculine. You're quite a masculine woman, aren't you?

K: Masculine. Very masculine.

B: She's got a very low voice.

K: It was a brief career but I really felt I learned a lot.

B: Was that your peak, do you think?

K: I think it was my peak.

B: Because you've gone downhill since then really, haven't you?

K: Quite radically.

B: Because you never get a chance to stand up or anything, you're always sitting down.

K: Well, that's the problem that we have, people behind desks. We sort of feel naked without a desk.

B: Yeah, in fact, it's rather uncomfortable you having one in bed at the moment, Kirst.

K: Well, the thing is that I can never get away from the feeling that I need a desk in front of me.

B: Yes.

K: Right? Goes everywhere with me.

B: Kirsty.

K: I thought you were going to call me Kirst?

"…you've gone downhill since then, haven't you?"

B: No, I'm going back to Kirsty because I'm coming round to a rather more formal question now. It's about *Breakfast Time* and your television commitments. You're sort of the new Frank Bough really, aren't you?

K: In a manner of speaking.

B: Yes. Frank's sweaters though, Kirsty. Victor is very interested in sweaters.

V: I am.

K: What in particular about sweaters?

V: Is it true that you get to wear all of Frank Bough's *old* jumpers?

K: Not all of them.

B: Oh dear.

V: Oh.

K: I don't get to wear the zip-up cardigans.

B: Well, you could never fit your radio mic properly, could you?

K: No, and anyway they're acrylic.

V: What about the Velcro ones?

B: You sweat with acrylic something terrible, don't you?

K: You can't wear acrylic under studio lights. It's just a fact of life.

V: Not with your oxters.

B: Just because we can see all that Amplex on the table there, Victor, there's no need to make assumptions about Kirst's…problems. But Kirsty, tell me, you then went and joined the BBC. You started in radio.

K: A great medium.

B: Well, we're on it right now! You went on television after that and then you went from behind the cameras into the front of them. How did you do that?

K: Well, I just sort of walked round.

V: Oh…

B: She's a wag, isn't she?

V: She's funny.

B: This is the Kirsty Wark you never knew.

V: I like her.

B: Do you?

V: I think I do.

B: Kirsty, your reputation in the media is one of a battle fighter. You really go for the jugular with your interviewees and you're doing something similar to us at the moment.

V: Bit of a vampire, really.

B: Yeah, a wee bit. But tell us, how do you do it?

K: What?

B: Interview difficult people. How do you get the nitty-gritty? How do you pin them down?

K: You do a lot of homework.

V: What? Algebra?

K: No, no… trigonometry.

V: Oh…

K: And then when you go into the studio you just make sure that you're going to say, well, this is what somebody out in the street would want to know from this person, and you make it your job to get the answer.

B: Do you ever have a row with them afterwards? Do they say, 'How dare you?'

K: Well, some people do say, 'I think you went over the score'.

V: Do they?

B: What do you say back? This is another side of Kirsty Wark. She mimed something there. Lucky this is radio, Kirsty, isn't it?

V: But have you got any make-up tips?

K: Well, yes, I have actually. The tea bags from this teapot don't just go in the bin.

V: Where do they go?

B: Oh? Where? Tell us. Do tell.

K: Most people would put them on their eyes.

V: But you put them in your armpits.

K: How did you guess?

B: Oh…

V: Oh…

K: That's not the only tip I've got.

V: Oh, there's another one.

B: Something a bit less personal.

K: No, no. The crumbs just get mixed up with a bit of water and these lines, these laughter lines…

B: Where?

V: Where are they? I can't see any lines.

K: These laughter lines, I just…

B: Pass me a magnifying glass!

K: A little bit of the gunge when you mix scone crumbs with some water, pop it on for the night and in the morning…

V: They've gone.

B: Oh, I see, pastry on your eye.

V: Super, shortcrust.

B: So, what's it like getting up so early? How do you get up?

K: How do you get up?

B: I sort of put my feet over the bed and there I am.

K: Well, I get an alarm call.

B: Oh, from the Beeb? From Auntie?

K: 'Time to get up. It's ten to four, it's time to get up.'

B: Oh, that's the middle of the afternoon.

K: No.

B: Oh, the morning. Oh, I see, of course. We're talking about *Breakfast Time*.

K: We're talking about *Breakfast Time*.

B: Oh right, yes.

K: Ten to four, I get a call.

B: That's atrocious. It's a long drive to London, isn't it? From Glasgow.

V: The coach is quite comfortable.

K: No, no. I prefer a car.

V: Do you?

K: Much prefer a car. Car picks me up here in Glasgow, twenty past four and I'm there.

B: What? For six?

K: No, for six the next morning.

V: Oh, of course.

B: I see what you mean. I was getting a bit confused there, Kirst. I didn't know where I was.

K: You've just dropped a scone on the carpet.

B: Have I? So I have.

K: I think you should pick it up.

B: Actually, it's not gone on the carpet, it's gone right down my jim-jams.

V: Stop searching for it, Kirsty.

B: I won't eat it, I'll just put it… have you got a receptacle I could use to…

K: There's the bedpan.

B: Oh, right.

K: If I could just say that it's way beyond my bedtime. I think I've given you enough of my time.

V: Do you?

K: I've got to think of what I've got to do in the morning.

B: And what you're going to look like, more importantly.

K: I think I'm going to have to clamp on my Walkman now, because I usually have bedtime stories to help me fall asleep.

B: Oh really? Oh, isn't that sweet?

V: That's super, that's cute. While we get dressed, Kirsty, why don't we read you one?

B: Why don't we talk to you and send you to sleep, Kirsty, because you've been nodding off a little during this interview already. You just settle down. I'll take your cup. There we are. Just put that right up to your neck, because we don't want you getting any chills.

(They tuck Kirsty into bed)

V: That's right.

B: No sniffing on *Breakfast Time*.

V: Now, once upon a time, there were two men called Victor MacIlvaney and Barry McLeish.

B: Yes.

V: And they became very, very mega-famous…

B: …and we never forgot our roots.

(We hear some more gramophone music as Victor and Barry creep out of Kirsty's bedroom)

V: Shh. Quiet! Don't wake her up.

B: Very quiet. Oh, mind that teabag there.

V: Well, she was very nice.

B: She was lovely.

V: Not like how she appears on television at all.

B: No, no… it's amazing what it does to you. And the futon was very comfy.

V: Yes.

B: Now careful with the door, Victor. Good night, Kirsty.

V: Good night.

(The door slams very loudly)

V: Oh, rats.

The End

1989

COMEDIANS: Victor and Barry at the Opera House

JOHN JAPES – SYDNEY SUNRISE – PEA PIES ROCKHAMPTON RHYMES

Forbes

On 1st January we got a message from the Sydney Festival organisers saying sorry for forgetting to invite us to the Festival New Year party. Yes, that was the bash we had seen in the distance, while feeling sorry for ourselves on the Opera House steps at midnight, like two Scottish Cinderfellas. However, we made up for not partying that night as Australia was basically just one party after another. Sydney is such an exciting city. *See Victor and Barry and Faint* was a huge hit there and we got invites to see other shows and to attend many other parties and events. We made friends with some of our stage crew and they took us out into Sydney to get a feel of the place. We went to Bondi Beach, swam in the sea and ate copious amounts of seafood.

Alan

Just before we left for Down Under, I finished the run of *Conquest of the South Pole* at the Royal Court. When we got to Sydney, I found out there was an Australian production of the play being produced at the Belvoir St Theatre. Not only that, but our lighting designer's girlfriend, Lisa Kelly, was in it!

The role I played was Slupianek, who led a group of disillusioned and dispossessed unemployed young men and becomes obsessed with an imaginary trip to the South Pole. The actor playing Slupianek in the Sydney production contacted me through Lisa and asked to meet up to discuss the role. I went to an

address in Elizabeth Bay to find him in a deserted, dark apartment, which he told me he was staying in temporarily. There wasn't even any electricity. I thought I was about to be murdered, but as you can see, I wasn't. This young actor, who for a second I suspected had lured me to this dank, dark flat to rob or kill me, turned out to be none other than Baz Luhrmann who went on to become the iconic director of *Moulin Rouge* and *Elvis* amongst others.

Forbes

Being a ginger in Oz did take a bit of getting used to. There was lots of info around at the time about a massive hole in the ozone layer over Australia, and everyone, not just gingers, needed to be very careful. Most days I was diligent and covered up and wore a hat. One day it was a bit overcast and I thought, 'Och, I don't need as much sunscreen,' and just slapped a little bit on. Later that night my back was bright red and I had a little white handprint where I had attempted to cover up. That was me telt.

Alan

I just remember walking down the street with strangers pointing at us and screaming 'skin cancer!' at the top of their lungs!

Forbes

The first night of our revised Australian show went really well. All the new jokes landed and we were very well received. Our hunch that 'there are Kelvin-sides everywhere' was correct and it was easy for people to relate to Victor and Barry's pretentions to poshness.

During one performance, there was a section where Victor goes in the huff and flounces offstage and through the audience. One night in Sydney, as I walked off, some people in the audience started throwing mints at me. I couldn't work out what was happening. Then I realised that as they were throwing them, they were saying in broad Australian accents, 'Minty....Minty....Crawford Minty!' They were referencing a character I had played in an episode of *City Lights* that had just aired there. It was weird.

After another show, we got this message that John Reid, one time manager of Elton John, had been in the audience. He thought the show was tremendous and wanted to invite us to a party at his hotel. Alan, Vivienne and I got in a cab that took us to the Sebel Townhouse Hotel, one of the most swanky, exclusive hotels in Sydney, which all the major rock stars stayed in when they played that city. There was a massive drunken party going on when we arrived, with the champagne flowing.

After one too many glasses, I ended up sitting next to Georgie Fame, trying to play the piano with him. But I was too far gone. We all thought it was time to go, but John was having none of it. He said we could all have a suite each in the hotel. We couldn't believe it. We had to take a special lift that only the VIPs could use to get to their penthouses. Once we got there, I seem to remember we tried to phone Elton, who was still in the UK, but he was out at the football! Alan got dressed up in some of John's jewels. Then everyone went to bed while Alan and I ended up skinny dipping in the outdoor pool on the roof. We watched the sunrise over the Sydney skyline. One of the most memorable nights of my life.

Alan

We went on a few TV news programmes to promote our show. One of them, *The 7.30 Report*, used a split-screen effect to show us genning up on Australian culture, with Victor and Barry sitting on a nearby sofa applying sunblock and slagging off everything we said!

The next stop on our tour was the Adelaide Festival Centre. We discovered to our horror that

Scots who tickle our funnybones

● **VICTOR AND BARRY** by Forbes Masson and Alan Cumming, The Playhouse, Sydney Opera House.

VICTOR And Barry could best be described as Scottish Hooray Henrys.

Fiercely proud of their Glasgow origins, they are touring "representatives" of the Kelvinside Young People's Amateur Dramatic Arts Society. Kelvinside, they say, is a sort of Glaswegian Vaucluse — with taste.

They look immaculate, with their slicked-back hair, navy blazers and Oxford bags, and their delightfully tailored speech is very funny.

The boys, who have changed their act since they were hits at the Edinburgh Fringe, home in on the Australian funnybone with panache.

Joyce Mayne, Kylie Minogue, our TV soapies and way of dressing are all wittily sent up.
— LINDA SMITH.

● Alan Cumming (Barry) (left) and Forbes Masson (Victor) — from cabarets and parties to theatre and television.

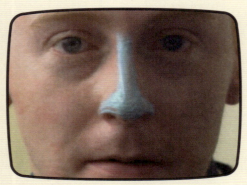

the Australian premiere of *Cats* was happening in the big theatre next door to ours, and as we walked through the backstage corridors to do our soundcheck we were accosted by Aussie musical theatre actors doing feline improvisations! The phrase 'try acting' may well have been muttered by both Victor and Barry *and* Forbes and Alan!

To get to our digs in Adelaide, we took a rattly old tram ride to a wee place by the sea called Glenelg. Our house was on the beach. The first time we got there we dumped our cases, jumped into our swimming togs and went splashing straight into the warm clear water. It was idyllic.

Whilst doing some press on a local radio show, one caller was an ex-pat who had a Scottish bakery in Adelaide and promised to send us some goodies. Sure enough, waiting outside our digs' front door the next day was a box full of pies, pineapple cakes, coconut snowballs, and loads of cakes you could get in a shop in Argyle Street.

Forbes

The Victor and Barry Show turned out to be just as popular in Adelaide. We had done our research there too, finding out local stuff we could take the mickey out of. The city was very welcoming and we were taken to a wildlife park to meet koalas, wallabies and emus. It's always great when you tour to places as a performer. It's much better than just being a tourist, because you meet the real people who show you the real place.

It was also in Adelaide where we found out about a local delicacy: the pie floater. This was, literally, a pie floating in a sea of pea soup, with the regulation tomato ketchup squirted on top. We realised we could make a gag out of that. Floaters existed in Scotland too, but we just cut out the middle man!

Alan

Many years later, when I was shooting *X2: X-Men United* in Vancouver, the late Barry Humphries came to visit us on set. I had shot the film Nicholas Nickleby with him earlier that year and we had got on like a house on fire, especially when I told him of my genuine love for pie floaters. So, knowing he was coming to visit, I asked the film's caterers if they could rustle up an approximation of this great delicacy. He loved it!

We had such fun being guests on *Touch of Elegance*, surely the campest show on Australian TV. It was basically a shopping show for middle-aged ladies presented by two middle-aged ladies Margaret Glazbrook and her sidekick Pam Ellis: V&B rechristened them as Margaret Elegant and Pam Not Quite So Elegant. On the show, we were flirty and dirty and a great time was had by all. Forbes even took down his trousers at one point to show Margaret his colourful Aussie shorts.

Forbes

The strain of the tour was beginning to take its toll, though, along with the heavy workload from the year before. In Adelaide, we came to the conclusion that it would soon be time to take a break from Victor and Barry. It was sad, but slightly inevitable. All good things must come to an end.

Alan

It had always been a juggling act trying to manouevre between doing V&B and our separate acting careers. I decided that when we returned to the UK, I would do *Knickers!*, a play I'd been offered at Bristol Old Vic, written by Carl Sternheim and directed by Steve Unwin who had also directed *Conquest of the South Pole*. That meant cancelling some Victor and Barry work, and that led to us deciding it was a good idea to take a break.

Forbes

However, there was still a lot of excitement and joy to come in Australia. We swam in the sea, we went to water parks, we saw the Australian version of *Les Misérables*. We saw La La La Human Steps, an amazing dance troupe from Montreal, and Barcelona's La Fura dels Baus who produce these huge public theatre installations. We went to loads of barbies and ate loads of shrimps, and we went to the cinema to see *Dirty Rotten Scoundrels*: when Michael Caine and Steve Martin emerged in dinner jackets and slacks, we thought that they had nicked Victor and Barry's image! But Victor and Barry were *not* dirty rotten scoundrels. They were Clean Ripe Gentlemen.

After Adelaide, we went to Alice Springs and climbed Uluru (also known as Ayers Rock). It was like being on the surface of Mars. In Cairns, it was so strange to be in a completely different climate. So humid. So oppressive. Thankfully our hotel had full air conditioning or we would have melted.

We got the chance to go snorkelling off the Barrier Reef with baby sharks and went through a forest where the trees were poisonous.

Our last port of call was a small town called Rockhampton. We met a lovely guy called Peter Mackay, a fellow ginger (or Blue as they say in Oz) who took us out to his holiday home on the coast and introduced us to custard apples. Peter was really taken by Victor and Barry, and has always kept in touch through the wonders of Facebook.

Alan

Also in Rockhampton we did more TV and had such a laugh with one of the local reporters, telling him our act was 'smut with witty lines; cheap but not nasty'. How true. We also performed our Australia song one last time…

*What's got sheep and what keeps us in
lamb chops?
It's better than Paris, it's the birthplace
of Rolf Harris!
What's got sun, sea and sand and koalas?
Can you guess where, there is no ozone layer?
You've had two hundred and one years of
Johnny Young
Dame Edna, Mad Max and Olivia Newton-John
We've come to tell ya, we like Australia
It's fairly dinkum to be on your soil*

Scots pair sure to take the mickey

Crazy Scottish comedians Victor and Barry will perform their special brand of humour in a cabaret setting at the Municipal Theatre for three nights during March.

Taking the mickey out of everything from Marks and Spencers department store to the Mahabarata, the pair kept audiences coming back for more at the 1988 Edinburgh Festival.

Rockhampton's fringe followers will get a chance to see why the duo are considered one of Britain's funniest acts when they perform at the Municipal Theatre on March 9, 10, 11.

As part of their first Australian tour, the pair of young Glaswegians in their monogrammed blazers and slicked-

stitches with the[ir]
thespian reminisc[ence]
worthy of Noel Co[ward]

Victor and Barry,
son and Alan Cum[ming]
studying up on A[...]
their show as relev[ant]
downunder audien[ce]

The pair have be[en]
British show busin[ess]
national treasures
the Edinburgh Fest[ival]

● Forbes Masso[n and Alan]
Cumming . . . Vi[ctor and Barry]

Forbes

And that was the end of the first part of Victor and Barry's trajectory. Alan and I came back to Blighty: me directly, Alan via Thailand. At the time, I thought that was it, and Victor and Barry were no more. I was low. Surprisingly, the next couple of jobs I got were basically double acts. Maybe I was trying to fill a huge Victor and Barry hole. The first was a play called *Loose Ends* by Stuart Hepburn.

It was about two young homeless lads and had a run at the Traverse during the Edinburgh Festival. I got to work with my great friend Stuart McQuarrie and it was directed by Ian Brown. We had a 10am slot and had to drink real cans of lager and eat Pot Noodle onstage. Ah, the trials of an actor. *Loose Ends* was well received and we filmed it in 1990. Then I played the part of someone else in a famous double act.

I performed as Stan Laurel, with Ronnie Simon as Oliver Hardy, in Tom McGrath's play about the legendary comedians. It was directed by my ex-flatmate Gerry Ramage, brother of John Ramage who played Mr Smee in the Peter Pan I did in Perth. We took Laurel and Hardy on tour around Argyllshire. Travelling in a Ford Luton Van, there were not enough seats up front for all of us, so we had to take turns in the back of the vehicle with the set. As the van wound round small one-track roads in the dark, it was treacherous holding on to scenery and costume baskets, trying not to get crushed. In one venue we

had to put 50p in a meter to get the lights in the small hall to come on. Despite this, the tour was a great success and we managed to secure more dates in less remote theatres.

In the autumn I did the best play I have ever worked on: *Cinzano* by Ludmilla Petrushevskaya. The director was Roman Kozak who came over to Glasgow from the Moscow Art Theatre and directed it for The Tron. He didn't a speak a word of English and we worked through a translator. It was a strange piece set in Brezhnev's USSR about three young men who get drunk on the only alcohol they can find: bottles of Cinzano. As they get drunker, their relationships to each other and the world are exposed.

It was funny, bleak, beautiful, violent and profound. I learned so much from Roman. His method of working was a revelatory experience. We were encouraged to semi-improvise, playing games with the text and each other. I had never felt so free onstage. I took that experience on into the rest of my career and it definitely made me a better actor. Our performances coincided with the Berlin Wall coming down. It was very special. It was not so much a double act, more a triple act! I still got to play piano though, and it was fantastic working with Peter Mullan and Paul Samson.

Alan

After *Knickers!*, I went to Stratford to join the Royal Shakespeare Company. But I had a pretty miserable time there doing *Singer*, a new play by Peter Flannery (who would go on to create *Our Friends in the North* for the BBC) that starred the late, great Antony Sher. I also played Silvius in a production of *As You Like It*.

I had wanted to join the RSC because I really liked the idea of being in a company for a sustained period; at that time, you signed on for a year of rehearsals in London, then runs in Stratford, Newcastle and London. I had done so many plays in Scotland that had runs of about a month, and I felt I was just getting settled into the character and the piece when it was time to finish. The thought of being with a group of actors and working on the same plays for a year was very appealing to me.

It just didn't work out that way though. I didn't enjoy the shows I was in, maybe because I didn't have enough to do in them. I felt I was in a sort of Shakespeare factory, just one of the cogs churning out theatre rather it being a living, evolving thing. It was also my first real time working outside of Scotland, and I'd also moved to London just before it started so I felt a bit rootless and lost. I have friends (Forbes principally) who have had many great experiences at the RSC. Actually, a couple of years ago I came to visit Forbes when he was doing a show at Stratford and it was kind of healing to see him doing great work there and enjoying it.

Forbes

The end of the decade may have seemed like the end of V&B, but 1990 was to herald a resurrection, with the cravates out, pressed and proud once again!

Kirsty Wark Remembers...

In December 1988, two very dapper young men came a-knocking, all cravates and Brylcreem. One was to become someone I see quite regularly on both sides of the Atlantic (indeed a very good friend) but never again have I had him in my bed, so to speak. Victor and Barry were coming to tea (Scones and Tea, in fact) and owing to the time of day and my type of work, I was somewhat fatigued; so we lay together on my candlewick, making a terrible mess with spillages and crumbs absolutely everywhere.

In the course of the conversation, I divined a not inconsiderable talent beside me on my bed. One a redhead, the other dark and smoky, like two fading Hollywood stars but yet so young and, well, perky! And so it has proved. I like to think I gave them both their first big break between the sheets. They certainly made my heart beat just a little bit faster.

1990

SODDEN SLACKS – SCOTCH SURREALISM HARNESS HEROICS

Alan

In 1990, Glasgow was made European City of Culture and Victor and Barry just *had* to come out of their self-imposed exile to let it be known that it was all down to them.

We were approached by the newly formed BSkyB channel (a result of the recent merger of Sky and British Satellite Broadcasting, which later became just plain old Sky) to appear on their topical sketch show *Up Yer News*. The show was produced by BSB's head of comedy Paul Jackson, who had produced *Red Dwarf* and *The Young Ones*, and they wanted us to make a video of a Victor and Barry song.

Forbes

We decided to do 'Kelvinside Men', and they sent a young director, Ashtar Al Khirsan, up to Glasgow to film it.

So, there we were in early 1990, dancing on location in Glasgow again, mercifully more or less on ground level this time. We played the piano in Princes Square shopping centre, we kicked some garden gnomes in the People's Palace, and we spun around in Kelvingrove Park throwing our hats in the air. Unfortunately, Victor slipped on the wet grass and landed in a puddle. His nice cream slacks were ruined. Mercifully, the wardrobe department had another pair, so filming could resume.

Alan

We really hit it off with Ashtar and had such fun being together again filming the song. My favourite parts were us walking along Dumbarton Road, miming as a speaker blasted the song, with old ladies out doing their shopping staring at us in disbelief as we pranced by. We also expertly guided the crew to a fish van nearby so that we could be literal when Barry sang the line 'I get fish from a van, I'm a Kelvinside Man.' And, of course, there was also a judicious use of a baked prop for Victor's line 'My loaf is a pan.'

In fact, we had such fun that we decided to get the band back together! We wrote a pilot for BBC Radio 2 called *Come Away In*, in which we expanded on the idea of real people having been members of the Kelvinside Young People's Amateur Dramatic Arts Society with V&B having catapulted them to stardom. In a caravan in their back garden (it was a radio show, remember!), Victor and Barry housed former KYPADAS members who had come back to Kelvinside for some respite from the hurly burly of showbiz stardom. In the pilot we had the amazing Barbara Windsor and Bonnie Langford as guests. They were both lovely and such troopers. While the pilot was broadcast, alas the series was not picked up.

We also decided to try and get a show together for that August's Edinburgh Festival. I say try because our schedules were pretty hectic.

Forbes

I filmed a TV version of *Loose Ends*, the Traverse play I had done the year before, and also appeared in an episode of Rab C Nesbitt. During Mayfest, I performed in *Elizabeth Gordon Quinn* directed by Hamish Glen, and also brought back Tom McGrath's *Laurel and Hardy*, taking it to the Tron in Glasgow and Assembly Rooms for the Edinburgh Fringe. I wrote and recorded a series of ten-minute semi-improvised sketch shows called *The Forbes Masson Half Hour* with Stuart McQuarrie and produced by David Jackson Young. They were surreal in the extreme. One sketch was about a small businessman who was big in Oban after exporting bottles of Scotch Breath. See? Surreal.

Alan

I was still running around the Forest of Arden in my Y-Fronts at the RSC, but soon was leaving to join the National Theatre to do *Accidental Death of an Anarchist* which I also adapted with the play's director Tim Supple. Luckily, I had a convenient gap in my RSC schedule so was able to come up to Edinburgh for the Festival.

Forbes

Our new Victor and Barry show idea was about their return from the Antipodean tour. We would call the show *Clean Ripe Gentlemen* after that idea we had when watching *Dirty Rotten Scoundrels* in Australia. The opening song 'High Caledonia!' was new but *not* a parody. After years of playing piano for Victor and Barry, I was getting a little more proficient on the keyboard and our songwriting was becoming a little braver. 'High Caledonia!' had a distinctive intro, consisting of us singing 'bap ba ra ra, bap bap ba ra ra' twice over a sequence of piano chords. We were to reuse this melody and the 'bap ba ra ra' in another song, a little later in our careers.

This is what I can remember of that short-lived song:

'Bap ba ra ra, bap bap ba ra ra
Bap ba ra ra, bap bap ba ra ra
Scotland is so nice to come home to
High Caledonia!
Scotland is a place we are prone to
High Caledonia!
We're very prone to ya!.........
We're back in the land of sgian-dubh and
Irn-Bru!'

We did a preview of *Clean Ripe Gentlemen* in Cumbernauld Theatre, before taking it to The Music Hall, the Assembly Rooms' biggest venue, and we sold out. Victor and Barry could still get those bums on seats!

We then brought the show for one night only to Glasgow at the King's Theatre. I think I did ten minutes of Rodney the Sex Machine, but Alan will know if that's the case.

Alan

It *was* the case! I remember it was so weird getting ready for Vic and Baz in the King's dressing room while hearing you onstage doing somebody else. And then the mad dash for you to get out of your Rodney drag and into Victor's slacks.

Masson about

The confessions of a Kelvinside comic

In 1982 TWO young students at Glasgow's Royal Scottish Academy of Music and Drama were asked to do a piece for the college cabaret. Neither had anything prepared, but they got together, came up with an idea and wrote a sketch called *Victor and Barry*. It worked like a dream.

The students were Forbes Masson and Alan Cumming and the show sent up two 'Am Dram' stars from Glasgow's posh Kelvinside. Eight years later the shows are still selling out. 'We never intended it to be anything,' says Masson. 'Now it's really bizarre to find that the characters are bigger than we are.'

It is to the credit of both men, then, that they have never let Victor and Barry take over. Both have been careful to develop other aspects of their careers. 'It's dangerous to start feeling safe and secure by doing the same thing over and over again, doing over and over again,' says Masson. 'You've got to try other things.' Hence his decision to do his own radio series, *The Forbes Masson Half Hour* (although each programme is only ten minutes long).

'The producer, David Jackson Young, wanted to do a comedy show that wasn't all belly laughs – the sort of thing you'd stumble across on the radio and not be sure if it was for real or not,' says Masson. 'It was also to be unscripted, so David would turn up at any flat with a tape recorder, we'd get an idea, and take it from there. Some of it is quite surreal and off the wall. Some of it's just off!'

A likeable, unpretentious man, Masson is also part of the newly established Actors Theatre of Scotland, which aims to give actors more say in what they produce. As with all fledgling theatre companies, funding is a problem. 'The usual way an actor works in Scotland is to get a job in the theatre, then try to get as many television appearances as possible to subsidise that. But one of the reasons we brought back Victor and Barry is because the standard of some of the television work in Scotland isn't very high,' says Masson. 'Working in subsidised theatre, debts begin to pile up, so I always see Victor and Barry as my way of sponsoring the arts!' **SALLY KINNES**

SEE HEAR IN SCOTLAND

The Forbes Masson Half Hour
Tuesday Radio Scotland

Acting up: comedian Forbes Masson in character and (inset) as himself

VICTOR & BARRY
ARE
CLEAN RIPE GENTLEMEN

KINGS THEATRE, GLASGOW
26th AUGUST

Forbes

We finished the performance and, as per every Victor and Barry show before and since, we had an encore song planned but thought we would do something extra special at the very end. I was wearing a harness like the one I wore in *Peter Pan*. At a certain moment I walked offstage to get hooked up to a line, and at the end of the song, Victor flew. I was way up high above Barry who looked bewildered and slightly pissed off. While the curtains were closed, I was hastily brought down from on high and I lay on the floor as if I had fallen. The curtains opened to reveal Barry with a large pair of shears and Victor flat out on the floor as if Barry had cut the line. It was very funny at the time.

And that was the total of Victor and Barry's stage appearances for the year, but it whetted our appetite to plan more for 1991. This time we would team up with Ashtar to help us write it.

In the autumn I filmed an episode of *Red Dwarf*, playing a wax droid of Stan Laurel. I also got a call from Gerry Ramage who was directing the Tron's Christmas show to see if I could take over from Bruce Morton, who I think had broken his foot. I had an afternoon's rehearsal and went on that night, playing opposite Dorothy Paul's Pirate Queen as her comic sidekick. Also in the show was a very young Ashley Jensen who was later to play my wife in *EastEnders* on the BBC and my girlfriend in *Catastrophe* on Channel 4.

Alan

As much as we were looking forward to doing another show together, I think we both felt that we needed to segue both ourselves and Vic and Baz onto something different. The new show would ultimately be a sort of Victor and Barry live show/sitcom hybrid, and although we didn't know it yet, it was truly to be their swan song.

Ashtar Al Khirsan Remembers...

I was working in the comedy department for Noel Gay Television when I first saw Victor and Barry. There was no other comedy act I'd seen that was so overtly, subversively camp and joyously political as Victor and Barry. At the time, comedy was dominated by heterosexual men with acts that were polemic in style and often delivered as a rant. Camp was a statement of intent in the '80s and '90s; it was yet to be monetised and sanitised.

Watching Victor and Barry nincompoop their way around life, I really felt that I was watching a subtle, charming but pointed challenge to everything straight and hetero. They spoke my language, a spiky, subversive camp, full of verbal excess and emotional outrage, tempered by an acute sense of their own ridiculousness. Victor and Barry's world was populated by characters with operatic delusions of grandeur. Queerness then was so undervalued and often reviled, it felt blindingly obvious that the only response was to give yourself an extravagant and histrionic sense of importance. It might sound absurd to Alan and Forbes but I did feel that they were an important part of a tribe of various outsiders and mavericks who populated my life at that time.

So when I persuaded my boss to let me go to Glasgow to make a video of

'Kelvinside Men', I think they were a bit bewildered about what it was all about. I was working on a news sketch show which was supposed to reflect current affairs. Victor and Barry didn't really fit into that category but I felt they were a comment on culture that was both very queer and very Scottish, neither of which had enough airtime, certainly not in England.

The video was a pure joy to make. I found the Hillman Imp for sale in Exchange and Mart and persuaded the owner to let me use it for the video. I have some vague memory of standing in a garage in Maryhill trying to explain the concept of Victor and Barry to the owner, and the fact that the Hillman Imp was their vehicle of choice.

Bizarre at it seems now, it was fashionable back in the '80s/ '90s for couples to put their names in big letters on their car windshield. A statement of coupledom and togetherness. I spent the night before the shoot cutting out Victor and Barry's names (though it needed to be 'Barry and Victor' because Forbes didn't drive back then). On the day of filming, I had to lie down in the back of the Hillman Imp pressing playback for the sound as Alan and Forbes drove around Glasgow singing along with the music.

That video is an early '90s capsule: buildings we filmed in are no longer there, fish vans have largely disappeared, and the people you see in the background represent a time that has completely vanished.

Observer Scotland Sunday 7 January 1990

ARTS

Mum approves as Alan keeps a better class of company

Barry, *sans* Victor, talks to PHIL PENFOLD about his work with the RSC.

IT SEEMS that Alan Cumming is fated. Every time his parents come to see a play in which he is appearing it contains bad language. Totally necessary to the plot, of course, and scripted by the author, but a bit risqué, nonetheless.

'All I do,' confesses the young Scots actor, 'is think to myself, "Well, here it comes and here it goes — — " and then you either get my mother making a very audible "Tch, tch, tch" noise in the auditorium, or saying — as she did once — "Oh DEAR! Alan!"

His ...

the board because there is a "concept" to a production from the director or the designer.

'It's rather odd going to Stratford when you've not been in these megaproductions before. Up until now, the theatre for me has been mainly small-scale stuff or studio performances. Underground material.

'In *Singer* [Peter Flannery's new play starring Anthony Sher] I don't really have that much to do in one chunk — I keep an entering in another new young man from another decade of the story. One of the reasons I wanted to join the RSC was because I wanted to do the classics. I've done a lot of new texts and translations of ...

All over Glasgow, the tea-room tinkle of silver spoons on fine china is being all but drowned by the braying of Victor and Barry's clones from Kelvinside

Let them eat cake: from left, Murray, Ryan and Cyril idolise Victor and ...

KELVINSIDE CAP

MURRAY STARES at the half-eaten box of chocolates in front of him, as he takes tea in De Courcey's Tearooms. 'Right. So which one of you has been at my Thorntons Continentals again?' His colleagues look guiltily at the floor. 'Don't look at me,' pipes Ryan. 'I've just had my teeth scaled. I'm on the herbal tea.' Reconciled, the boys begin to talk about their holiday plans. Sighs one: 'It's so difficult to find a decent geranium sitter these days.'

These are the V and B Boys, taking their name from the comic double act Victor and Barry who specialise in sending up the middle-class Young Fogey contingent from the more desirable districts of Glasgow. The V and B Boys look, walk, talk and even *think* like their heroes. They videotape every Victor and Barry show on TV, and attend all the gigs, singing along quietly to every song. It's an unofficial, yet demanding, fan club.

The cult characters themselves were created 'one afternoon in a cupboard', while actors Forbes Masson (Victor) and Alan Cummings (Barry) were still at the Royal Scottish Academy of Music and Dance. Now Victor and Barry, the twee dahlings of Kelvinside, have reached international status with tours in the States and Australia as well as regular appearances on STV, *Night Network* and Radio 4's *Loose Ends*.

Their success lies in the fact that the comic duo are a welcome novelty among the Eighties' parade of agit-proppers, rebel rousers and downbeat self-deprecators. With their brilliantined hair, monogrammed blazers, cravats and Oxford bags, the two boys come from the privileged and dotty world of the Kelvinside Young People's Amateur Dramatic Arts Society with egos that far outstrip their talent.

'Victor and Barry are would-be's, trying their best. There are a lot of people like that, not being themselves but what they think they ought to be,' Alan Cummings explains. 'Like my first landlady in Glasgow. She used to spray me, the cooker *and* my food every morning at breakfast.'

The V and B Boys also live in an air-freshened environment. After years of struggling with monosyllabic Lloyd Cole lookalikes, the Hillhead landlady mafia have taken the boys to their bony hearts. 'This waistcoat? Mrs McGilvray gave it to me when her second cousin died,' says one.

'As you put the ... mannerisms ... be witty in a ...

Life, apart ... University, is o ... boys meet to ... bitch about al ... they remain s ... little piece ... England'), w ... Glasgow that ... Kelvin Bridg ... town with g ... pavement'). ... milieu' that ... various bec ... rooms who n ... after hour o ... tea, reciting ... *Song* to one ...

A likely ... tea-room, ... faced, the re ... After he ha ... says deris ... when he w ... has the ch ... group sur ... standards ... last break ... bill. Bung ...

REPORT B ... PHOTOG ...

Scones and Tea

with Ian Hislop

When Victor and Barry met Ian Hislop for an episode of their BBC Scotland radio series *Scones and Tea with V&B*, he was relatively newly minted as editor of the satirical magazine *Private Eye*. Owned by Richard Ingrams (characterised on their pages as Lord Gnome), the publication was home to many regular features such as Street of Shame, which highlighted the ignominies on Fleet Street. But Victor and Barry remembered a younger and even shorter Ian from his cub reporter days in Kelvinside, long before he had earned his 'most sued man in Britain' soubriquet.

Victor: Hello there, fans.

Barry: Victor and Barry here.

V: On the streets of London, Soho.

B: We are indeed. And this week, in our series of in-depth probes into our former members …

V: … of the Kelvinside Young People's Amateur Dramatic Arts Society

B: … yes, yes, we'll be meeting someone rather special, won't we, Vic?

V: Uh-huh! The editor of that wonderful gardening magazine, *Privet High*.

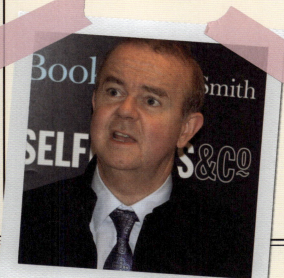

B: Yes. Now, do you think this is the right place?

V: Well, there are lot of bags of compost out here.

B: Oh, yes. And I can see a nasturtium through that blind.

V: Oh, good. Let's go in.

B: Watch out for that dung!

(We hear some old gramophone music; Victor and Barry are now inside the offices of Private Eye magazine)

B: OK, speak into the microphone, tell us who are you and what you had for breakfast.

Ian Hislop: My name is Ian Hislop and I'm afraid I didn't have any breakfast.

V: You're on a diet, are you?

I: No, no, no. I just missed it.

V: Well, can I make a suggestion? I think you should be.

B: Now Victor, stop it. Have a scone, Ian.

I: I think in response to that, I'll have two.

V: What do you take in your tea?

I: What do I take in my tea?

B: Yes. Is that a difficult question?

I: It is. I think I'm not familiar with the vernacular 'take in your tea'.

V: Sugar!

I: Oh, I see. I see. What you put in your tea.

B: It's not my accent, it's your ears!

I: Just a little sugar. That's lovely.

V: Right, there you go.

B: Tell us about *Privet High*. When did you first become interested in gardening?

I: *(spluttering his tea)* Sorry about that. I have absolutely no interest in gardening at all.

V: Really? Oh.

I: And never have had.

B: So, there's no gardening at *Privet High*?

I: No gardening at all.

V: What about the gnomes?

I: There are a few gnomes in there, but no gardens.

B: So what it is it about?

I: It's about scandal, really. About jokes, gossip, journalism.

V: Like *The Sun*?

I: Sort of like *The Sun*, except with longer words.

B: Of course, we remember you from many, many, many years ago, don't we, Victor?

V: Yes, we do, when you were one of our prodigies.

B: That's right. You were a hack on the *Kelvinside Gazette*. Remember?

I: Oh, yes, my early days.

B: That's right. Yes! You used to write a column called *District of Shame*, revealing scandal in Kelvinside.

V: Remember that time you came along to review the show and we dragged you onstage?

I: It was very embarrassing.

V: That wonderful, wonderful American musical called *South of Chiswick*.

B: Yes. We were a bit short. And as you were quite short, we thought we'd have you. *(Victor and Barry laugh)* I don't mean to be heightist, but you really are.

V: You're a funny man.

B: I am, actually, aren't I? Talking of height, Ian, you are quite small. Is that good for peeking through keyholes and things like that, finding out scandal?

I: Not really, because I don't do any of that.

B: No? Are you sort of the boss?

I: I suppose that's it, really. Yes. I sort of sit there and read it.

V: You're young to be the boss, aren't you? You're quite young.

I: Yes, I suppose I am a bit.

B: And you're quite small. How old are you?

I: I'm 13.

V: Is Richard Ingrams your uncle?

I: No, he isn't.

V: Oh, so that's not how you got the job then.

I: No, he's my father.

B: Ah, that's it. That's it.

V: He's small as well, isn't he?

I: He is 6ft 2".

V: Small for a tall person.

I: You could work here. You're very good at facts.

B: And so, is he dead?

I: No. I believe he's still alive. He's in the country, though.

B: I see. So, you kind of ousted him from his position of power and took over *Privet High*?

I: I suppose you could say that. He did gracefully leave, so there wasn't a lot of ousting to do.

V: Another cup of tea?

I: I will, thanks, yes.

B: Super. Here's another scone for you to keep you going. Do you want one?

I: No.

V: Go on. Dip it in your tea. You're at your auntie's.

B: Now, in your capacity as a hack on the

Kelvinside Gazette, you must have seen some wonderful shows with us, which we've done.

I: Yes, I saw the great Renee, or Renée, Roberts.

V: Renee. Her acute is silent.

B: Really? Did you see her?

I: I saw her in *Hello Renee*, which was amazing.

V: She was super in that one. It was a pity about the plaster cast.

I: She did awfully well with it, though.

V: I mean, she coped amazingly, didn't she?

B: Yes. We had to cut the walk down the stairwell, but apart from that …

I: I didn't even notice.

B: Well, there you go.

I: *Brigadoon*.

V: *Brigadoon*. Currently running in London. Not half as good. We've seen it. It's crap.

I: The trouble about the West End is it doesn't have that sort of calibre of performer, does it?

V: You're talking about the West End of London, not the West End of Glasgow, of course.

I: Oh, yes. Yes.

V: What other shows did you see with us?

I: I saw *Perchance to Dream*.

V: Did you like that?

I: I loved that. The chorus was so right, somehow.

V: I don't think we actually did that one, Ian.

I: Perhaps I just imagined that one.

V: Perhaps you did.

B: Did you ever see *Call Me Madam*?

I: *Call Me Madam*.

V: Madam! Oh, he's laughing now! Did you see that? With Renee?

I: I think I missed that one. Was that her finest hour?

B: One of them. One of them. Except actually, she didn't make it on the first night. Remember that? She had an accident in Presto's. And Ophelia … do you remember Ophelia? Did you not have a thing with Ophelia?

V: She remembers you, Ian.

B: She was our wardrobe mistress. You were always complimenting her frocks.

I: Oh!

B: I can see you remember now.

V: She's still got the scars.

B: Now come on, stop crying, Ian.

I: Right.

B: You alright?

I: Sorry, I was just rather moved by the thought of Ophelia.

B: Well, she is moved by you too. She tells us all the time. Actually, she doesn't, because you know what?

I: What?

B: She's dead.

Barry:
"She died"
Ian:
"Oh, that
is funny"

V: She died.

I: Oh no!

B: She died.

I: Oh, that is funny.

B: It's not funny at all. She dived too deep in an artificial water tank we had for a production of *Jaws*, and she got the bends and died.

I: That's terrible.

B: Yes. I should say, viewers, that we are actually in the *Private Eye* office.

I: This is the joke room you're in. This is where everyone comes to make the jokes.

V: Yes. The flock wallpaper's a bit out of taste, really.

B: Who sits over there?

I: Over there?

V: Mm-hmm. That small seat there.

I: The small seat over there is for Peter Cook.

V: Oh, him. Yes.

I: Who sort of owns the magazine.

B: He owns the magazine?

I: He does. Well, he's the major shareholder. 75% of the shares are his.

V: Oh, so it's privatised.

I: It is privatised.

V: *Private Eyezd*! Now, over there, is that where your lawyer is?

I: The lawyer does come up here, yes. This is where he reads the magazine before it goes out to check that there's nothing defamatory in it.

V: Doesn't do a very good job obviously then, does he?

B: Suits, Ian.

I: Suits.

B: Mm-hmm. Libel suits.

I: Oh, sorry, not Jonathan Ross-type suits.

B: No, no, no, no. Libel ones. You get a lot of those, don't you?

I: We do get a lot of those, yeah.

B: Why?

I: Well, we print things that people don't like.

V: Lies, you mean.

I: Some of those. No. We print things that people decide are not true. And then we have to test whether they are or not. And if they're not, we have to pay them huge amounts of money.

B: And you pay them yourself, out of your own pocket?

I: I don't, no.

V: Because you're dressing rather shabbily today. I just wondered why.

I: You think this is shabby? I dressed up for you.

V: Did you? Really? You shouldn't have bothered.

B: Of course, you do have Scottish roots, don't you? And that's very apt for an editor of *Privet High*. Roots.

I: Roots. Yes. My father was Scottish.

B: Really?

I: And I spent a few weekends in Scotland when I was younger.

V: So you've got whisky in your blood then.

I: Very much so. I feel it is part of me.

B: Good. Good. Are you thinking of returning to Scotland when you grow up?

I: I was, actually.

B: Were you?

I: Yes. I mean, house prices being what they are, I thought I could perhaps sell my flat here and buy Stirling or something like that, and commute down.

V: Yes. Lovely castle.

B: Yes. That would be nice.

I: It would be very nice.

B: You must come and interview us again when you get back up to the ain country.

I: I'd love to.

V: Bring your own scones the next time, though.

(We hear gramophone music, with Victor and Barry back out on the streets of Soho)

B: You know, Victor, I think that went quite well.

V: Mm-hmm.

B: I'm sure that when this interview comes out, the sales of *Privet High* will pick up immensely.

V: Yes, but do you think we can sue them?

B: Possibly. He was rather rude about Ophelia, wasn't he?

V: What's our lawyers number again?

B: We'll have to get a new one. He's dead.

The End

1991

SWEATY SIGN CHER'S SHARE BUFF BOYS LENNY HENRY PURCELL

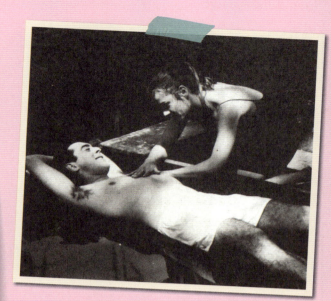

Forbes

In early 1991, I took the production of *Laurel and Hardy* to the Wellington Festival. It was strange to be going back to the other side of the world with another double act. We played the Paramount Theatre there for a week and then I went off touring the South Island on my own with a backpack the following week. I had never done anything like that in my life before.

At Mayfest, I went back to the Tron to play Claude, with John Stahl playing my father and Ashley Jensen as my sister in *The Real Wurld?*, Michael Boyd's version of Michel Tremblay's fantastic play *The Real World?*

It was here I got to work with the extraordinary and brilliantly funny Bob Carr for the first time. After Mayfest, we took the production to the Long Island Arts Festival in America. Michael asked me to write a Christmas show on my own, so I started work on my first version of *Jack and the Beanstalk*, with original songs in the style of Victor and Barry. That year, I got the chance to play Stan Laurel again. This time as a wax droid in the cult sci-fi sitcom, *Red Dwarf*.

Alan

Things went a bit nuts for me this year. I started it off playing the Maniac in *Accidental Death of an Anarchist* at the National Theatre, and a couple of months later I won an Olivier Award for my performance. Soon after that, I flew to the Czech Republic to start shooting my first feature film, *Prague*, playing opposite the French screen siren Sandrine Bonnaire and Swiss legend Bruno Ganz. Later, I filmed the Christmas classic *Bernard and the Genie*, written by Richard Curtis, in which I starred as Bernard opposite Lenny Henry (little did I think I would be in the *Bernard and the Genie* Hollywood remake 32 years later, this time as the evil boss Rowan Atkinson played in the original!).

I finished off 1991 playing Romeo at the National Theatre studio, with Sophie Thompson playing Juliet.

Forbes

In June, I went to visit Alan in Prague. We started work on another Victor and Barry show which we had decided would be the last. We hoped it would lead to a TV series for the Kelvinside pair, and Ashtar Al Khirsan (the director from *Up Yer News* who shot our 'Kelvinside Men' video) came on board as script editor. She also appeared onstage with us, briefly.

Alan

I sent one of the Czech film drivers to pick Forbes up from the airport and gave him a sign to hold up that said, 'ma bum's aw sweaty!' He immediately knew this was his ride!

When I got back to Blighty we guested on *Paramount City*, a variety show for BBC1 that featured the best of British and American comedy, recorded in an old studio in Soho that had once been the notorious Windmill Theatre, home of the nude tableaux vivants. We actually appeared on an episode alongside David Bowie! Alas he wasn't there when we recorded our bits. However, we did see Cher, who was shooting for an earlier episode in the series, during one of the more fallow periods of her career. I remember that when she left, her people had taken all the flowers and the vases they were in, and even the complimentary cookies and the plate they were on!

In the Scud turned out to be Victor and Barry's farewell show. Of course, they had been saying farewell practically from the time of their inception. They wore nostalgia as a badge of honour, yearning for the past. Like Cher (though actually *way* before Cher), they always hinted that their current show would be the last one, effectively creating the idea that they too would soon become part of their own nostalgia. This was the blurb for their show that opened Mayfest at Glasgow's Theatre Royal in 1988, less than a year after their first ever TV appearance:

Yes, it's true. The party's over. The lights are going out all over Kelvinside, and there will no doubt be tears before cocoa as Victor MacIlvaney and Barry McLeish say adieu in melodious moments and melancholy meanderings.

But there was also a practical element that infused Victor and Barry's constant teasing of their imminent demise: we had other jobs. Victor and Barry were constantly in danger of taking over our lives. As much as we loved them and loved *being* them, as the song says, we had a lot of living to do. Perhaps because they had been created for a one-night-only event at our first-year college cabaret, they had an inbuilt obsolescence, and part of their charm (or arrogance) was that they knew audiences wanted them to keep going; making every new show a potential farewell was both a tease and an affirmation.

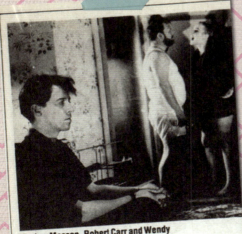

Forbes Masson, Robert Carr and Wendy Seager in The Real Wurld

Forbes

As the title suggested, this new show would be Victor and Barry stripped bare, with stories of their origins. It was also a tie-in for marketing reasons. Both Alan and I realised that to get anywhere in the Edinburgh Festival with such a huge number of performances happening at the same time, our posters had to stand out. We had to delve into dodgy areas. We had to hire a fly-poster guy. Though 'illegal', this act was a total necessity for all shows, and we had to supply these guys with several large posters which they plastered all over premium sites in the city.

In previous years, we had chosen a picture of Victor and Barry emulating the iconic image of the masks of comedy and tragedy. But for 1991, we wanted something different, something that would catch the eye. We decided that a show in which Victor and Barry revealed all should not only be called *In the Scud*, but the poster image had to be of Victor and Barry naked. Obviously, obscenity laws would not allow us to expose the Kelvinsiders' generous and, in one case, gingery genitalia. We didn't want our pubic area in the public arena, so we had the show's title plastered across the picture to cover our modesty. We got the fabulous and acclaimed actor David Morrissey, Alan's pal and neighbour in Crouch End, to take photos of us in our pants.

Alan

My brother lived in Edinburgh at the time and I got a call from him one day just before the Festival saying he had nearly crashed his car on his way to work at the sight of a giant Forbes and me splashed across a billboard, in the scud!

We worked really hard on the script. I think it is the most structured and elaborate thing we ever did for a live show. After Forbes came to visit me in Prague, he, Ashtar and I all met up again in Cambridge when I was shooting *The Last Romantics*. I was staying in a new hotel and there were a few teething troubles with the service. For example, I was awakened one morning by the front desk saying, 'This is your 6.30am alarm call, 15 minutes late!' One night when we were writing in my room, I was a bit peckish and opened the minibar to get a snack. But all did not seem well as I began to munch and discovered that what I was imbibing was way past its sell-by-date. It was the final straw. I snapped. Forbes and Ashtar still rib me to this day because I immediately picked up the phone, called reception and said, 'The nuts in my mini bar are off!'

VICTOR and BARRY

IN THE SCUD

Assembly Rooms, Edinburgh
11th-18th August   6.30 pm
Kings Theatre, Glasgow
25th August   7.30 pm

David Morrissey Remembers...

I'd known Alan for a while before I met Victor and Barry. We were neighbours in London and I'd go and hang out with him and his wife at their flat. They were wonderful, happy days. At the time, I was working sporadically as an actor, mostly in the theatre, and so had to supplement my income with a bit of photography on the side. I did portraits and publicity shots for actors and had a fairly decent camera.

One night I went over to Alan's for supper and Forbes was there. The two of them were just hilarious. I could hardly eat my food for laughing. They were discussing their up-and-coming Edinburgh show, *Victor and Barry: In the Scud*. I offered to take the publicity shot.

The next day I arrived at Alan's and went out into his garden to set up. The plan was to shoot them as if they were naked except for their signature cravates. It was a typical North London ground floor flat garden, overlooked by many other homes in the surrounding street.

Victor and Barry came out, with just cravates and very short undies to protect their modestly. We managed to secure the cravates to a wall with some cotton so it looked like they were being blown in the wind, and V&B pulled shocked faces at being caught in the buff as I snapped away.

The house behind Alan's was having some work done, and after a while I became aware of some sniggering laughter behind us. I looked up to see several builders on scaffolding pissing themselves at the sight of two semi-naked men with slicked-back hair and silk cravates, their undies up the crack of their bum, being photographed by a gruff Northerner shouting, 'This way! Work it boys! Work it!' V&B were oblivious to the audience they'd attracted. Then one of the builders shouted, 'Nice arse!'

Alan and Forbes leapt ten feet in the air and ran screaming into the kitchen. I tried to persuade them to come back outside and finish the shoot but they wouldn't do it. They were mortified, and none of us could stop laughing. I was so nervous I hadn't got the shot. But once I developed it, I saw that there was one frame, maybe just before they'd heard the 'nice arse' shout, that was perfect.

I was so pleased with the finished poster, V&B in the middle looking outraged by their own nakedness, the cravates perfectly floating in the wind, with VICTOR AND BARRY across the top, and IN THE SCUD strategically placed at an angle across their crown jewels. I think that was my only brush with greatness as a photographer. Sadly, after that my acting career took off and I had to ditch my dream of being the next David Bailey.

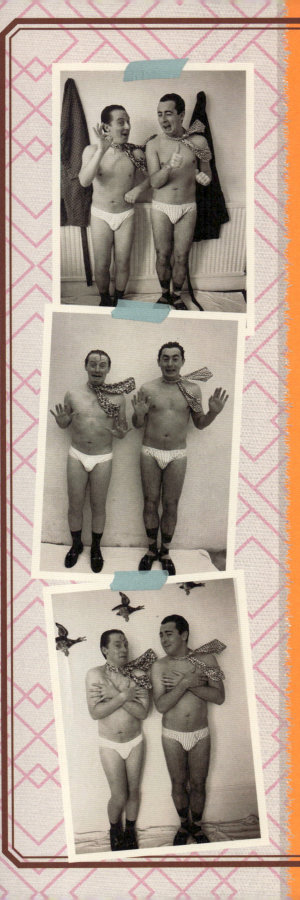

In the show's first ever preview at the Tron Theatre, Ashtar actually appeared as Victor when Forbes was offstage getting ready to re-enter as Angora O'Rourke, one of Victor and Barry's neighbours. This was achieved by Ashtar wearing an identical Victor ensemble complete with a motorbike helmet to cover her face (the helmet had been kindly lent to us by the singer Jimmy Somerville!)

The combination of Ashtar being somewhat shorter than Forbes as well as utterly terrified, and the audience being totally confused by the whole idea ensured that this part of the show was cut immediately. Jimmy's helmet was returned.

Forbes

In the Scud was a success, and after our previews in Glasgow and Cumbernauld we went on to perform it at the Assembly Rooms during the Fringe, before returning to Glasgow for a one-nighter at the King's. Later in the year, we performed a short run of the show at the Purcell Rooms on the South Bank in London as part of the Perrier Pick of the Fringe season.

I remember Lenny Henry coming to see it there while Alan was filming *Bernard and the Genie* with him. He spoke to me afterwards but I really couldn't concentrate on what he was saying to me. Firstly, because he was so famous, but also because I was shocked at how tall he was, towering above little shorty me. I do remember him saying that he loved the show, but wondered how much life the characters would have. It was something I was thinking about too.

In the Scud was more like a little play, much more formed than our usual shows. It had an actual story for the first time, and telephone interruptions from their agent Clorissa and KYPADAS goddess Renee Roberts. And finally, of course, it featured their actual demise. But the old Victor and Barry were still very much present: there were also set-pieces that not only did nothing to further the plot but actively slowed it down. Here's one of them, the story of how Victor and Barry met…

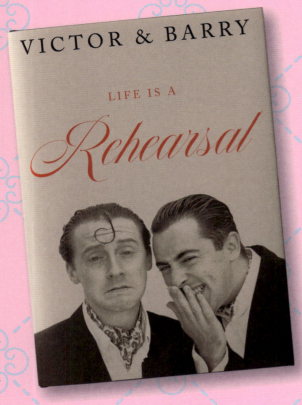

VICTOR & BARRY

LIFE IS A

Rehearsal

VICTOR
Yes, tonight is the night that we reveal all.
Fasten your seatbelts for the rollercoaster
ride to the kernel of the nut that is Victor
and Barry.

BARRY
We will now read excerpts from the
unabridged and unexpurgated version of our
autobiography. *Life Is a Rehearsal*. Picture
the scene, if youse will. We go back into the
midst of time…

VICTOR
Back, back, back to 1746.

BARRY
Not that far back, Victor. Back to nineteen
fivvvvvvvmnnb.

VICTOR
Back to the King's Theatre, Glasgow and Wendy
Craig's stunning portrayal as Hedda Gabler in
Ibsen's *The Seagull*.

BARRY
Just as she let rip with the automatic
firearm at the end of a rather overwritten
act five, we hear simultaneous screams from
the audience of, 'Is there a doctor in
the house!?'

VICTOR
'Is there a doctor in the house?…'

BARRY
'My waters have broken…'

VICTOR
'My waters have broken…'

BARRY
…I said simultaneously.

VICTOR
Yes, ladies and gentlemen. That night,
Lucretia McLeish and Hortense MacIlvaney were
in the theatre.

BARRY
My mother sat on a plush top-price seat in
the circle.

VICTOR
My mother sold programmes at the back of
the stalls.

BARRY
They never met.

VICTOR
But who could have guessed…

BARRY & VICTOR
But who could have guessed…

VICTOR
…that their offspring, which would so
quickly burst forth into the world, would be
so strangely linked and so ruddy talented.

BARRY
So what did happen that evening? Well
after my mother's waters broke, she
apologised to the people next to her for

the mess. She was helped out of her seat and was escorted to the taxi rank outside where a luxurious limousine smoothly whisked her off to her private hospital.

VICTOR
My mother staggered up the stairs to the main door and tried to hail a fast black but was pushed to the ground but a large Italian-looking lady who was climbing into a luxurious limousine. My mother suffered a broken arm.

BARRY
When my mother arrived at the Muriel Grey Memorial Hospital

VICTOR
Muriel Grey, sadly…

V&B:
…still with us.

BARRY:
She was popped into a wheelchair and swished into the operating theatre. Just as my father arrived to record the event on his cinecamera, the first and only child of Lucretia and Luigi McLeish was born. Smiling and yes crying – but many said that cry sounded uncannily like the opening aria of *Seven Brides for Seven Brothers* as sung by Howard Keel.

VICTOR
After lying on the ground for ten minutes, my mother stood up only to be knocked down by my father, who arrived in his rusty car. He opened the hatch back and shoved my mother in. En route to the Maryhill workers Maternity Clinic and Poor House, disaster struck: the fan belt broke. And just as my father was pulling off my mother's tights to replace it, out popped me onto the back seat and hence I was named after that car, a Vauxhall Victor estate.
In later years I dropped the names Vauxhall and Estate to become known as simply Victor. Although there were few present at my birth, a traffic warden, Mme Saffron Chapeau, a French Canadian, swears blindly that she heard me whistle 'A Spoonful of Sugar' as I entered the world.

BARRY
I had a very happy childhood. My mother adored me and showered me with gifts and instilled in me my everlasting love of musicals. My first words ages six months were 'More… now'. My father ran an ice-cream empire, and although he delighted in testing new flavours of ice cream on me with a funnel and taking me into the shed at the bottom of our landscaped garden and letting me play with his collection of extremely sharp knives, which he used for gutting ferrets, he was essentially a distant man.

VICTOR
My father too was a distant man. This is because for half of the year he lived in a different country. Partly due to his work commitments, but mostly due to the fact that he hated my mother and my ten older sisters and me. The main love of his life was gravestones, which he made and sold for a living. Consequently, our house was full of reject stones converted into household items such as a dining-room table, toilet seat and stairs. His love of stone was such that he names my ten sisters after various types. They are called, in descending order of age; Jade MacIlvaney, Turquoise MacIlvaney, Marble MacIlvaney, Amethyst MacIlvaney, Slate MacIlvaney, Onyx

MacIlvaney, Terracotta MacIlvaney, Granite MacIlvaney, Zirconia MacIlvaney and Fran. She's a brick. We lived together in a rather cramped two bedroomed prefab with a lot of cupboard space but only six power points.

BARRY

Our spacious villa was also inhabited by our family lodger, Grigor Bartholomew, an ex-US service man from Minnesota. He worked as a door-to-door electrolysis and waxing operative but was always on hand to supply the emotional and spiritual splint to the fractured family life we experienced. Uncle Grigor was also indispensable to my mother often coming home in the afternoons to help her with her household duties. Sometimes he would come home twice in the afternoon. Uncle Grigor was like a father to me: he was forever having shipments of Bazooka Joe bubble gum sent over from the US – my favourite.

VICTOR

When I was five, my father's business suffered a setback, which meant that cash was tight and therefore my mother couldn't afford to buy me a new uniform for my first all-important days at primary school. However, my family's motto, 'When in doubt, improvise,' came to the rescue and my mother rather skilfully doctored some of my older sisters' pinafores to fit me. This proved confusing to my teacher however as she was always putting me in the girls' team for Time and Tune. This left a large stain on my persona; school was not easy for me. I was bullied by my classmates on a rota system. They would taunt me by calling me Speccy four-eyes, Joe 90, Pinz-nez pus. This affected my eyesight, and a year later I was fitted with spectacles. The bullying continued but was confined to a verbal nature. Indeed, only once was I attacked physically – I was pushed to the ground by a dark-haired Italian looking child who smelt of ice cream. I suffered a broken arm. I had few friends.

BARRY

I bought lots of friends at school. I had a very magnetic personality, still do, and of course the abundance and easy access to

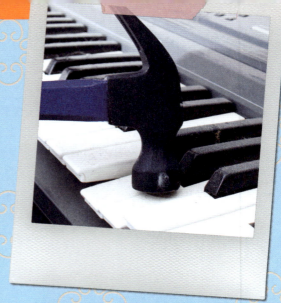

my father's ice cream helped my popularity enormously, so much so that when I formed a gang the demand to be in it was so great that I had to hold auditions. Children had to be excellent in one theatrical skill and au fait in another two. It was at one of these auditions that I first met Victor.

VICTOR

I didn't get in.

BARRY

My main influences at the time Magdalene De Menthe, my piano teacher who had a huge emotional influence on my life. Her motto: 'Be proud, be loud,' I have never forgotten. She was a strange fish in that she wasn't a fish, she was a woman. She never married, she had a skin head and she smoked cheroots. It was the discovery of the latter that decided my mother to discontinue my lessons, which is the reason for my somewhat rudimentary piano technique, as you witnessed tonight.

VICTOR

My biggest influence was my art teacher, Rab MacFayden. Thanks to him I now understand what it is to throw the perfect pot. My other influences include Valerie Singleton, Lionel Bart and Flipper. I was a straight-A student when I first sat exams in high school, but a freak accident involving a netball made me vulnerable to dizzy spells and forgetfulness which resulted in my work going…

BARRY
…Downhill.

VICTOR
Downhill. However, my fall from academia
was mirrored by the realisation of my true
vocation. I auditioned and got the lead in
the school's production of *Godspell*. The
local paper said: 'Christ was almighty'.
I was spotted by a talent scout from
Crackerjack Young Entertainers and was asked
to audition for the programme. I decided that
I would sing 'Mother of Mine', the Neil Reid
hit. However, the day before the audition
during a particularly boisterous PE double
period I slipped on some ice cream and
broke my arm and was
therefore unable to
audition. I cried a lot.

BARRY
Owing to the last-minute
indisposition of one of the
auditionees, I was able to
be seen for Crackerjack
Young Entertainers. I sang
'Mother of Mine' the Neil
Reid hit. I was then asked
to appear on the programme.
However, on the way home
from the audition I was
attacked by ten red-haired
girls. My injuries denied
me the chance of appearing

in front of millions on the actual programme.
Despite this setback, I threw myself into the
Kelvinside social whirl, dating a string of
girlfriends all of whom developed terrible weight
problems due to excessive ice cream intake.

VICTOR
Two weeks after the auditioning fiasco, my
mother received a singing telegram. It was from
my father, who was in Cairo. The singer sang
that my father had invented a revolutionary
new way of engraving of stone called the
Horace Tool. He had just patented it and was
set to become a millionaire. The singer sang
all that to the tune of 'If I Were a Rich Man'
the Topol hit — that's Topol the singer, not
the toothpaste. That was a red-letter day.
For eighteen months I became a new person,
confident, assured and, well, a bit flash. I
had feminine callers every hour of the day.
I learned to drive, I learned to use other
golf clubs and I threw away my glasses and got
contacts. For once in my life I was popular.

BARRY
Mr Tragedy came a-knock-knock-knocking on
our porch fly screen when I was fifteen. Five
years earlier my Uncle Grigor had disappeared.
My mother told me that he had gone on a long
journey, but I had thought the reason for his
swift exit had been the ready availability of
home waxing kits from high street chemists
leaving him semi redundant. However, I was to
be proved wrong that dreich summer afternoon
when Detective Sergeant Guy Wersch of
Kelvinside CID stood on our Welcome mat licking
one of my father's 99s. It transpires that
Uncle Grigor had been discovered at the bottom
of the River Kelvin with his feet encased in
concrete — the same concrete that my father had
used to build an extension to our barbecue five
years earlier. My father was arrested, charged
and found guilty of indecently assaulting
Uncle Grigor with his electrolysis equipment…
to death. This was a terrible time for me as
my father wasn't allowed to continue running
his business in Barlinnie. It meant that I got
no pocket money and therefore I lost all my
friends. I tried to run away but the police
found me in a taxi asking the driver to take me
to *Brigadoon*.

VICTOR

My eighteen months of hedonistic joy were
brought to an untimely end with the
revelation of a design fault in the Horace
Tool. It could only spell E before I except
after C. The model was withdrawn from
the market. My father was sued and lost
everything. A broken man, my mother kicked
him out. I was feeling particularly low when
I met and fell in love with Angora O'Rourk,
the Irish American wool heiress. I sent her a
letter, it said, 'She read it; she chucked
me; I drank.'

BARRY

I attended Kelvinside Technical College where
I studied for and HND in Hotel Management.

VICTOR

I drank…

BARRY

During this time, my mother and I were
moved from our villa, forcibly, into a more
snug bungalow. I graduated from college
and I converted the bungalow into a deluxe
executive B&B establishment for single
gentlemen.

VICTOR

I drank…

BARRY

Meanwhile, my father was studying for
a degree in sociology and sculpture in
Barlinnie and his sculptures sold for huge
sums of money. I saw none of it. He went on
to become the subject of a South Bank Show
and he published his autobiography, *From Mint
Choc Chip to Marble*. Neither my mother nor
myself were mentioned in this book.

VICTOR

I couldn't get through the day without a
snowball over my muesli…

BARRY

I finally left home when my mother married one
of our house guests 30 years her junior.

VICTOR

In an attempt to ebb to rising flow of debt
accrued during my eighteen months of almost
heaven, I secured a job as junior manager
of the high fashion Scholls Department of
Milngavie Remedial footwear. I still drank.
Then one drizzly Thursday the door of the
shop opened…

BARRY

…ting-a-ling…

VICTOR

…and in walked a tall dark handsome stranger,
and next to him stood Barry.

BARRY

I was returning a pair of defective flip-flops.

VICTOR

And as he reached for his receipt in the
pocket of his poncho

BARRY

…It was in the '70s…

VICTOR

No, it was raining. Out popped a ticket for
that night's performance of the Partick Hill
Players production of *I don't Want to Rumba
in Rio, I'd Rather Limbo in Largs*, which I
was going to see too. I then put my glasses
on and Barry recognised me and gave my arm an
affectionate thump for old time's sake.

(Barry thumps Victor's arm)

BARRY

We arranged to meet that evening and
discovered that we shared a like-minded
interest in all the aspects of show business,
drinking, accruing wealth and…

BARRY & VICTOR

…telling lies.

BARRY

And we've never looked
back since.

VICTOR

Well, sometimes…

Scones and Tea

with Nicholas Parsons

The last of the Kelvinside Young People's Amateur Dramatic Art Society alumni that Victor and Barry visited for their BBC Radio Scotland series *Scones and Tea with V&B* was the late, great showbiz legend Nicholas Parsons. After leaving Kelvinside, Nicholas started out as an actor but moved into comedy and presenting, becoming the resident comedian at the Windmill Theatre in London's West End, famous for its revue shows and nude tableaux vivants. He was the host of BBC Radio's *Just a Minute* for over 40 years but is perhaps best known for ITV's *Sale of the Century* with its haunting opening announcement of 'and now, from Norwich… it's the quiz of the week!'

Barry: Now, Victor.

Victor: Yes, Barry?

B: Can you guess who our guest is today on *Scones and Tea with V&B*?

V: Oh, no. Give me a clue?

B: OK then, he used to live in Norwich.

V: Norwich. Right.

B: When we phoned him up to ask him to be on the show he said, 'Now just a minute!'

V: Just a minute? Oh right, right, right.

B: He's suave, he's sophisticated, he's elegant.

V: What's his name?

B: Nicholas Parsons. Oh, rats!

V: Got you.

(We hear crackly gramophone music. Victor and Barry are now in the hotel room of Nicholas Parsons)

B: Right, now. Speak clearly into the microphone, tell us your name, what you do for a living and what you had for breakfast.

N: Victor and Barry, I didn't expect this from you. You know from our past association exactly who I am.

B: Come on. Say who you are, what you do for a living.

N: Victor and Barry, you know perfectly well who I am. That is why you've come up here to my hotel room and you know the reason you're here is because of our close association from our past …

B: Exactly.

N: … in Kelvinside.

V: Exactly.

N: When I lived in Byres Road.

B: Exactly.

N: Roxburgh Street.

V: He remembers.

N: Number 15, Roxburgh Street.

V: You'll have guessed now, ladies and gentlemen, this is Nicholas Parsons we're talking to.

B: Nicholas Parsons.

V: He hasn't introduced himself.

B: He's refused to introduce himself.

V: He thinks everyone knows his voice.

B: Nicky, listen, we met you … can I call you Nicky?

N: You used to, years ago, when we were in the Kelvinside Players together.

V: Oh, Big Nick we used to call you.

B: Getting back to the point in hand, you were a student in Glasgow, remember? An engineering student. And do you remember you came to the Kelvinside Young People's Amateur Dramatic Society, first of all as a sort of engineering consultant, and you actually built the ship for *Show Boat*. Remember that? Wasn't it a lovely ship?

V: All these fanny things at the side, beautiful.

B: Fanny things?

V: Sort of flippery things, the things that drove the show boat …

B: The sort of wheels. Remember that?

N: And do you remember the big laugh when it sank, and you went down?

V: Oh, funny!

B: Those were the days, weren't they?

N: It was my ad-libs that kept the show going, I remember, entirely.

V: It was.

B: It was.

N: Entirely.

V: You played the quizmaster in that production, if I remember rightly.

N: Quizmaster?

B: Mmm hmmm. We wrote it especially for you. The quizmaster on the show boat.

N: You think that was the first experience I had of that line of work?

V: That's how it all happened, don't you remember? That's how it all happened.

N: You were really seeing my future.

V: That was it. We didn't have enough money for the production, so we had a fundraising event. We had the car boot sale of the century, and that was it!

B: And you were tremendous at it. You really were.

V: You went onto that programme, anyway, what was it called? *The Price is Right*?

B: No, *Sale of the Century*. That's 'from Norwich'; that's what we're talking about.

V: 'The quiz of the week.'

B: Could you bung me over another scone there, please, David. It's David, our little producer. We're supposed to pretend he's not here, but he is. Do you want another scone, Nicky?

N: No, I've had quite enough, thank you very much.

B: Victor? Do you want another scone?

V: Ah, why not, why not. Hang the hips.

B: That's it.

N: Do you think the listeners will understand you when you've got a mouthful like that?

V: Well, they know me, you see; they know me.

B: They know we're having scones and everything here, and packing our faces. Now, Nicky, you came to us with a silly English accent, and we drummed that out of you. Remember that show?

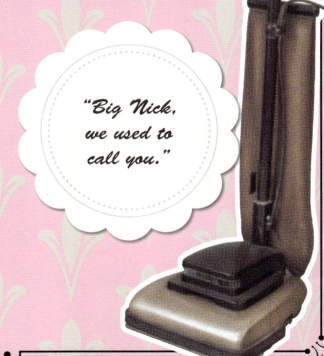

"Big Nick, we used to call you."

N: Well, you see, I had been to an English public school and that gave me, in those times, a very English sort of way of speaking. And then I came up here and I had this sort of trauma shock when I bumped into the two of you.

B: But remember that show we did, *Pygmy Lion*. It was when we were working on your accent, and you played the part of … well, in the play it's originally Eliza Doolittle, but we changed it, as it was you playing that part, to Elijah Doesabit.

N: Oh, Elijah Doesabit.

"*Tell us about when you were a nude comic…*"

B: Remember that one? And we worked on your speech impediment in that show. Art was imitating life, really.

N: It really was, because I did have one when I was very young. I used to stutter very badly.

V: I've still got one, Nicholas, it's my teeth. And the scones, yes, and the seeds from the raspberry jam that my mother made.

B: Beautiful jam. Who wrote *Pygmy Lion*, Victor?

V: George Bernard Matthews.

B: That's right. Remember George Bernard Matthews, Nicky?

N: I thought it was Noel Bernard Matthews.

V: It might have been. The turkey burgers in the lunch room were superb, weren't they? Remember that?

B: Oh, delicious time we had. But you left us, if you remember, Nicky. You left the West End of Glasgow, and you moved unfortunately south.

N: Only professionally.

B: Tell us about those days in the Windmill, Nicky, when you were a nude comic.

N: A nude comic.

B: Did you just stand there, take your clothes off and tell jokes? Is that true? Or did you just stand there?

V: You didn't need to write a script.

N: To try and put the facts right, the comedian at the Windmill, and I was the resident comedian for six months, always followed the fan dance.

B: Fan dance. Now, what's that?

N: Well, that's …

V: Air conditioning was it, perhaps?

N: No, it's where girls have fans made of feathers, and they try and move them delicately. And in those days a girl could take her clothes off on the stage, but she mustn't move. So you could have a nude, but if she moved it was rude. During the fan dance there was always a girl on a pedestal at the back of the stage; and there was a classic occasion, when she was on this pedestal, quite still, and the poor girl got a fit of the coughing and everything began to shake. It got the biggest round of applause I've ever heard in the theatre.

V: Really, I bet.

N: We actually had to bring the curtain down.

B: Oh, I've just dropped …

V: Dropped his scone.

B: Sorry about that, Nicky.

V: All on the carpet, Barry. Can't take him anywhere.

B: I'll get it later.

V: Skelt his tea as well.

N: There is a hoover in the cupboard, by the way. I asked the maid to leave it because I knew what a couple of messy twerps you were.

V: Well, thanks for that

B: Tell us, Nicky, you've been a star for a long time now.

N: Well, I thought you'd never mention the word.

B: Tell us about your hair, Nicky.

N: Well, I could take it off and show it to you, but …

V: No, it's all your own! It's all your own! You don't rent it.

N: No, it has stayed, which has been a great help to me, professionally.

V: And it's a pleasure to see that you haven't done the Crowther on it.

N: The Crowther?

V: You know, game show hosts, they try and disguise their looks, and it's dreadful, it's dreadful.

N: No, well I don't know what to say about all that. I think I'll just sit back and take the compliments.

B: I like your cravate best of all. You got that idea from us, didn't you?

N: Well of course, I've got to admit that.

B: Yes.

N: I am trying to bring the cravate back. Because you're working very hard, I think, too.

V: We're doing our best.

N: I think there's only three of us left, but it could happen.

B: This is it.

V: We're a triumvriviate … I'm trying to say a triumvirate.

B: Never buy teeth from a catalogue, Nicky.

V: No.

B: Never buy them from a catalogue.

N: No, well you see I used to play the cravate types on the stage as a youngster, you know: 'who's for tennis?' The frightfully English juveniles, but I feel they're all part of my theatrical …

V: Heritage. Paraphernalia. The heritage comes from you. You pass it all on.

B: Are you ever going to come back to Kelvinside, Nicky?

N: Oh, every time I go to Glasgow I pay a sort of sentimental return visit to Kelvinside.

B: You never come and see us.

V: You always avoid us, why's that?

N: But the thing is, I still haven't finished what I tried to say: because of this incredible training … no, no, please! Don't look like that, Victor. Because of this incredible training, this early experience, it gave me the confidence to step out as an actor and a performer, as a straight man, as a dame in pantomime, a quiz show host. I've done that, and I owe it all to you, Barry, and to Victor.

V: About time you said it, Nicholas. It had to be said.

N: Well, it's wonderful to have this opportunity to publicly declare my indebtedness to you.

V: Nicholas, thank you very much.

B: Bless you, Nicky.

N: Victor, Barry, what can I say? I shall always remember those incredible days when the three of us worked together in Kelvinside.

V: Marvellous. I'm moved. Oh, just turn the tape off.

(The interview is suddenly cut off and we hear some more crackly gramophone)

B: Oh, drone, drone, drone. That man could talk the hind legs off a goat.

V: Exactly, if we hadn't pulled the plug out he would never have shut up.

B: Oh, I know. I thought, surely he was going to bring it out?

V: What?

B: The big red book.

V: Oh, you mean *This is Your Life*?

B: I thought it was a pure set-up for, 'This is your life, Victor and Barry.' I did.

V: I'd love to see my great uncle from Reykjavik.

B: Oh, and my relations in Zimbabwe are gasping to see me apparently.

V: Never mind, tomorrow's another day.

B: That's right. You never can tell, as George Bernard Matthews said.

V: Mmm hmm.

The End

SCUDDING SITCOMS – PIANO PRANKS
B&B OR NOT B&B

Alan

The idea behind making *In the Scud* much more of a narrative-based, structured show was that we wanted to write our own sitcom and so were trying to attract the attention of TV bosses. At least, I think that's what we wanted. More likely, it was the logical progression for comedy acts of the time and we just went along with it.

Translating Victor and Barry to the small screen, however, proved to be rather more difficult than either of us thought. First of all, we weren't TV sitcom writers… yet. And even the stuff we had written for TV was very theatrical and performative: two words that to this day can make the saltiest old TV producer dogs shake in their boots. But we have never believed that just because the screen is small, we have to be!

Forbes

Scottish Television had asked us to try to write a Victor and Barry-centric sitcom for them in 1988 and we came up with a murder-mystery musical called *There's Somebody Dead in Our Baby Grand*, set in (where else?) Kelvinside! Although it featured the orange-skinned travel-show presenter Judith Chalmers being found deceased in a piano, as well as several literal red herrings, it got no further than the treatment stage. Also, STV never made a sitcom… ever.

THERE'S SOMEBODY DEAD IN OUR BABY GRAND

TREATMENT FOR SCOTTISH TELEVISION

BY

ALAN CUMMING AND FORBES MASSON

SUGGESTED CASTING

OF

CHARACTERS

VIOLA TUCH......................UNA MACLEAN
RENEE ROBERTS...................DOROTHY PAUL
RUARI BLACKLAWS.................ARNOLD BROWN
OPHELIA WISHART.................MYRA MCFADYEN
LANCE BARCLAY...................JACKIE FARRELL

EPISODE ONE

OPENING SHOTOF SOMEONE (UTTERLY FAMOUS) SMILING

MANICALLY

THEN WE SEE A GLOVE, DROPPING THE LID OF A BABY GRAND

PIANO THEREBY COVERING THE CELEBRITY'S FACE. (I.E HE

OR SHE HAS BEEN DEAD INSIDE THE PIANO ALL ALONG.)

CAMERA SHIFTS TO REVEAL A PAIR OF HILL-CLIMBING BOOTS.

CAMERA NOW TAKES MURDERERS (WEARER OF HILL-CLIMBING

BOOTS) P.O.V.

WE THEN HEAR LAUGHTER AND CHATTER IN THE DISTANCE.

THE HILL- WALKING BOOTS START TO MOVE IN QUICK

SUCCESSION AND WE HEAR THE MURDERER'S HEAVY BREATHING,

NAY, PANTING.

JUST AS THE MURDERER REACHES THE FRONT DOOR THE

LAUGHTER AND CHATTER BECOMES VERY LOUD AND WE HEAR A

KEY TURNING IN THE LOCK. THE DOOR OPENS. THE BOOTS

OWNER ARE TRAPPED BEHIND IT.

THE CAMERA LIFTS AND WE SEE OUR TWO HEROES...

VICTOR MACILVANEY AND BARRY MCLEISH

ENTER THE HOUSE THROUGH THE DOOR-WAY. THEY ARE D[...]

IN BURBERRY MACKINTOSHES AND ARE IN MID-SENTENCE

VICTOR: SO I JUST SAID 'I'VE NEVER SEEN NASTURS[...]

GROWN THERE BEFORE'

BARRY: YOU'RE SUCH A GAS, VICTOR

VICTOR: YES, I KNOW. DON'T PUT ME NEAR NAKED [...]

THE AUDITION PANEL BEGINS TO ARRIVE, DEPARTING INFO [...]

THE FORTHCOMING SHOW. IT IS TO BE 'SONGS FROM THE

SHOWS', A JAMBOREE, A MUSICAL MELEE. I.E. BITS FROM

LOTS OF MUSICALS.

THE PANEL ARE........

RENEE ROBERTS, GRAND-DAME OF THE SOCIETY, AND LEGEND

IN HER OWN LIFETIME

RUARI BLACKLAWS, LEADING BARITONE AND SLIGHTLY

PSYCHOTIC BUTCHER

OPHELIA WISHART, FUSSY, NEUROTIC WARDROBE MISTRESS,

WHO HATES THE SOCIETY MEMBERS AS THEY MUCK UP HER

COSTUMES.

LANCE BARCLAY, OUTRAGEOUS AND PETULANT CHOREOGRAPHER

OF THE BUZBY BERKELY SCHOOL.

VICTOR AND BARRY TO CAMERA: THERE'S SOMEBOD[...]

OUR BABY GRAND!!!! IT'S JUDITH CHALMERS (O[...]

THEN WE HEAR A SCREAM FROM THE KITCHEN.....

VIOLA HAS JUST FOUND AN AUDITIONEE DEAD, STABBED[...]

BARRY: QUICKLY! LET'S GO TO THE POLICE. GET OUR

COATS FROM THE CUPBOARD

VICTOR OPENS THE CUPBOARD AND ANOTHER DEAD BODY FALLS

OUT.

BARRY, TO CAMERA: THIS IS GETTING TEDIOUS

[...]E. WE SEE BARRY GOING INTO THE

[...]. WE SEE HIS HAND TURNING ON THE SHOWER.

LOTS OF SHOTS OF THE SHOWER SPRAY A LA PSYCHO. THEN WE

SEE A REVERSE ANGLE, FROM INSIDE THE SHOWER CURTAIN.

A RED-HAIRED FIGURE APPROACHES, WITH HIS HAND HELD

HIGH....LOTS OF SCARY MUSIC. THE FIGURE MOVES RIGHT

UP TO THE SHOWER CURTAIN AND PRESSES HIS FACE AGAINST

IT. WE SEE THAT IT IS VICTOR!!!

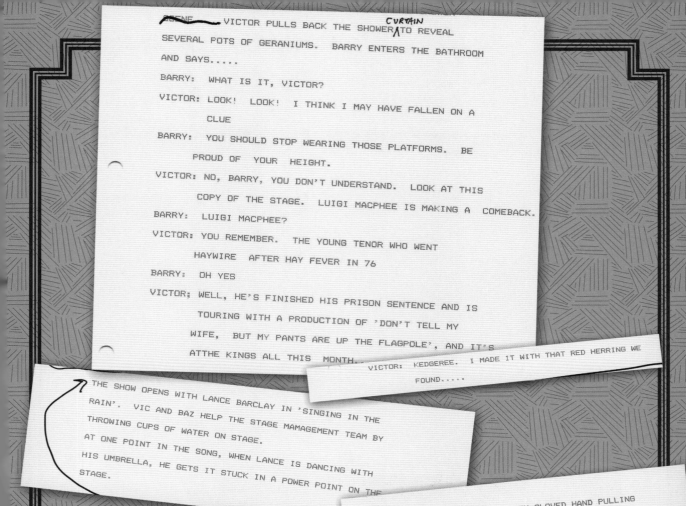

SCENE _____ VICTOR PULLS BACK THE SHOWER ∧CURTAIN TO REVEAL
SEVERAL POTS OF GERANIUMS. BARRY ENTERS THE BATHROOM
AND SAYS.....

BARRY: WHAT IS IT, VICTOR?

VICTOR: LOOK! LOOK! I THINK I MAY HAVE FALLEN ON A
        CLUE

BARRY: YOU SHOULD STOP WEARING THOSE PLATFORMS. BE
        PROUD OF YOUR HEIGHT.

VICTOR: NO, BARRY, YOU DON'T UNDERSTAND. LOOK AT THIS
        COPY OF THE STAGE. LUIGI MACPHEE IS MAKING A COMEBACK.

BARRY: LUIGI MACPHEE?

VICTOR: YOU REMEMBER. THE YOUNG TENOR WHO WENT
        HAYWIRE AFTER HAY FEVER IN 76

BARRY: OH YES

VICTOR: WELL, HE'S FINISHED HIS PRISON SENTENCE AND IS
        TOURING WITH A PRODUCTION OF 'DON'T TELL MY
        WIFE, BUT MY PANTS ARE UP THE FLAGPOLE', AND IT'S
        ATTHE KINGS ALL THIS MONTH.

VICTOR: KEDGEREE. I MADE IT WITH THAT RED HERRING WE
         FOUND.....

THE SHOW OPENS WITH LANCE BARCLAY IN 'SINGING IN THE
RAIN'. VIC AND BAZ HELP THE STAGE MAMAGEMENT TEAM BY
THROWING CUPS OF WATER ON STAGE.
AT ONE POINT IN THE SONG, WHEN LANCE IS DANCING WITH
HIS UMBRELLA, HE GETS IT STUCK IN A POWER POINT ON THE
STAGE.

WE THEN SEE THE MYTERIOUS OVEN-GLOVED HAND PULLING
DOWN A LEVER, AND LANCE IS ELECTRIFIED ONSTAGE. HIS
DANCING BECOMES RATHER FRENETIC THEN HE DROPS TO THE
FLOOR. VIC AND BAZ ARE IN THE WINGS, WATCHING

VICTOR: I JUST DON'T KNOW WHERE THAT MAN GETS HIS
         ENERGY FROM

BARRY: HE'S ABSOLUTELY ELECTRIC
THEY THEN REALISE WHAT HAS HAPPENED AND RUSH ONSTAGE,
PRETENDING IT'S ALL PART OF THE SHOW.

Add: Finally, the culprit is u...

THE AFTER-SHOW PARTY CHEZ VIC AND BAZ. ALL THE
REMAINING SOCIETY MEMBERS ARE THERE. VICTOR AND BARR...
ARE DOING THE BIG PERRY MASON NUMBER, ROLLING OFF THE
CLUES AND THE EVIDENCE. LOTS OF CLOSE-UPS OF NERVOUS
PEOPLE. AT THE END OF THEIR SPEECH, THEY ACCUSE EACH
OTHER SIMULTANEOUSLY.

VICTOR: DON'T BE RUDDY RIDICULOUS, BARRY

BARRY: I! I AM BEING RIDICULOUS?

VIOLA: YOU'RE BOTH BEING RIDICULOUS. IT WAS ME! I
         KILLED THEM!

VICTOR: YOU, VIOLA? BUT WHY? YOU ALWAYS SEEMED SO
         HAPPY, SO STURDY

BARRY: YOU'RE AN AVID READER OF THE PEOPLE'S FRIEND

VIOLA: EXACTLY. THE PEOPLE'S FRIEND. EVERYBODY'S
         FRIEND. VICTOR AND BARRY'S FRIEND. SO WHY
         DID YOU NEVER GIVE ME A PART IN ANY OF YOUR
         SHOWS? FOR YEARS I'VE WANTED A PART. BUT YOU
         IGNORED ME. EVEN WHEN I KILLED OFF HALF THE

```
        COMPANY YOU IGNORED ME.  THAT'S WHY I DID IT.
           TO GET BACK AT YOU FOR HOLDING ME BACK,
           DENYING  THE  WORLD OF THE GREAT TALENT OF VIOLA TUCK
      SHE IS DRAGGED OFF BY THE POLICE, SINGING 'SUICIDE SAL'
      BARRY:    I THINK SHE WAS BEING A BIT EXTREME.  WELL,
                I'M  GLAD THAT'S OVER
      VICTOR:   WELL, LET'S NOT LET A FEW MURDERS SPOIL THE
                FUN.  LET'S PARTY!
      THEY KNOCK BACK THEIR CAMPARI, THEN BOTH GASP
      VICTOR:   THIS TASTES POISONED
      BARRY:    OH, SHE WOULDN'T
      VOILA BURSTS IN THE DOOR AGAIN, CRYING 'OH YES I
      WOULD'.
      VICTOR:   BUT, VIOLA.  ONE THING IS PUZZLING ME.
                WHY DID YOU KILL JUDITH CHALMERS?
      VIOLA:    I ALWAYS HATED 'WISH YOU WERE HERE'
      SHE IS DRAGGED AWAY
      VICTOR AND BARRY GO THE PIANO AND SING THEIR SWANSONG.
      AT THE END OF IT, THEY BOTH SLUMP OVER THE BABY GRAND
      THE PARTYGOERS GIVE THEM A STANDING OVATION.  THEY GET
      UP AND DIE AGAIN........


                      THE END
```

Alan

Cut to 1992. We were older, wiser, and coming to the end of Victor and Barry's life as stage characters. We were ready to move them into another sphere. Although it turned out that we needed to change not just the sphere but also the characters themselves, we had a lot of fun coming to that realisation.

Forbes

As you can see, we had trouble with a title. *V&B's B&B*, *Digs*, *Victor and Barry's Bed and Board*, *Victor and Barry Give Bed and Board*, and *Victor and Barry's B and B* were all mooted, but the title on the script eventually sent out by our agent was *V&B's B&B: A Comedy of Good Manners*, with the first episode entitled *Look Back in Angora*. Yes, Victor and Barry now had a fancy London literary agent and we were starting to take this writing lark seriously.

But interestingly, and perhaps not coincidentally, we were taking Victor and Barry out of Kelvinside and transplanting them into some generic English seaside town. This concession was no doubt at the behest of our agent or some TV executive, worried about our humour translating or travelling south.

Gone is the Kelvinside Young People's Amateur Dramatic Art Society and all references to the horrors of East Kelvinside being mistaken for Maryhill. Instead of the past glories of various KYPADAS productions, we now have theatrical themes of the various rooms in this guest house.

Alan

Vic and Baz are still tangentially involved in amateur dramatics, however, with an equally bonkers group

of misfits as their theatrical tenants. In the treatment, some of their former am-dram cohorts have somehow been magically transplanted south, though they are no longer specifically sons and daughters of Caledonia. So, Lance Barclay, their choreographer, is now a bona fide Cockney; another example, no doubt, of us being told we'd only get a show made if it was less Scottish. We were both still in our mid-20s at this point, relatively new to the (for us) complicated mores of London's TV comedy scene, and so we did what we were told.

Forbes

The result is still pretty funny but definitely a little more generic and lacking the Victor and Barry authenticity. Looking back at this document (which hopefully was only a rough draft considering the many hilarious spelling mistakes like 'Glenead Jackson', though 'Bonnier Langford' is surely the definition of a happy accident), it's funny to see how we took some of our past, real-life experiences and added them to the V&B world. So, Agnetha Nils, our Swedish exchange student and goat-loving chambermaid in this new boarding-house setting, was based on the German girl who was our unexpected flatmate when we first performed the Victor and Barry show in London; we also wrote a part for her in the mock-documentary *Victor and Barry Take the High Road*.

Alan

We also seem to be very down on Kenneth Branagh, and who knew Barry was responsible for all Ken Dodd's Inland Revenue woes?! Finally, Harry Lauder's ghost was not once aping on the strains, but appearing once nightly on the stairs!

Clare Grogan Remembers...

I'm an enormous fan of silliness, so Victor and Barry were right up my street. Silly they may have been but there was also a cleverness that made them the legends they very quickly became in Glasgow in the '80s. I remember being excited to even walk past them in the street. They were so brilliant at capturing a very familiar type of Glasgow character, but best of all was getting to witness how much fun on stage Forbes and Alan had being these two devilishly daft divas.

```
                    V AND B'S B AND B

                           OR

                          DIGS

                           OR


           VICTOR AND BARRY'S BED AND BOARD

                           OR

          VICTOR AND PARRY GIVE BED AND BOARD

                           OR

            VICTOR AND B ARRY'S B&B
```

Randolph Havergal-Kerr — An aged character actor who, apart from a brief stint in "Softly Softly" in 1972 playing the part of Charlie Pigeon O'Toole the cheerful yet psycholgically scarred police informer, never really made it. He has an amazing capacity for drink, and when inebriated loves to regale other guests about his laddish exploits with other famous alcoholic stars.

The Bunting Triplets — a trio of faded songstresses — Poppy, Bunty and Ruby. Their looks are going, their voices croaking, but they are still on twice-nightly at the Winter Gardens.

Lance Barclay — a cheerful cockney handyman and odd-jobber. Also, in contrast to his hefty physique and gruff manner, he choreographs Victor and Barry's amateur shows. "Very light on his feet for an obese man".

Renee Roberts — the grand dame of the amateur world, Renee, the bubbly divorcee is also Victor and Barry's rival in the B&B world, as she has recently opened up guest house in a more favourable area of town. Her house has a view of the beach— something which makes V&B very bitter, as they fear this could lose them some trade. Their envy of Renee's location is complicated by the fact that they both harbour very romantic longings for her, though they keep these very secret.

The Olivier Suite
Supposedly, as V&B would have it, the great man spent a weekend in this twin room with ensuite bath, researching his role in John Osbourne's "The Entertainer". Vic and Baz have decorated the room accordingly, down to the minutest detail, including a selection of false noses and hump casts from some of Larry's famous roles

ranagh's basement

he least enticing room of the house, and only used as a ast resort — a dark and dank single in the bowels of the arth. This is a bit of an in joke between Victor and arry, as they see Kenneth as a bit of an upstart, a atcherite money-grabbing shyster who can only give one erformance(and a very noisy one at that) who sold out to he Americans instead of serving his time doing the unds of the regional reps and guest spots on Inspector rse. V&B's motto has always been "Learn, learn, learn"

Viola Tuck — their next door neighbour, a constant shoulder on which they regularly cry. Viola is a Spanis civil war veteran, and has many bits of shrapnel buried amidst her varicoses which she willingly shows anyone wh stays still long enough.

Brenda Turk — local gypsy tea-leaf readerextraordinaire and new-age guru, Brenda is on hand to administer to Vi and Baz's spiritual needs. She also sometimes parks he caravan in their garden.

Victor and Barry's guest house is merely a semi-detach villa in a run down street quite far from the town's promenade. But to V&B it is a palace, the last bastic of the heady days when British touring theatre was "alive". Each room has its own character, specially designed by the pair in an overtly theatrical extravag manner. It is all rather faded, however, and a bit sa

Examples of rooms —

Jackson's Chamber

Gleaned spent four months in this particular room whe she played in weekly rep. Victor maintains that his catching her unaware in the shower prompted her to disrobe in her later films. The room is in Elizabeth style, paying homage to her magnificent role of our troubled ex-monarch.A recent addition to this room ha been a copy of the Labour party manifesto and severa dozen plastic red roses

Doddy's dining room

The great Ken Dodd used to sit in the dining room whi on tour and bemoan the fact that no matter how hard worked he never had enough money. It was Barry who suggested to him the "McLeish Method" of banking, na sticking half of your earnings under a mattress and calling it expenses

Langford's Lounge

A vast ballroom (6' x 10') with a pay as you view Bush monochrome portable in one corner, and a raised "stage area" with baby grand in the other. It is here, come Saturday night at around 11pm that guests are politely forced to view Victor and Barry's candlelit revues. It is named after Ms Bonnie Langford, as it was here, believe V&B that the toothy showbiz star did her first splits at age 2 and a half. Victor was holding her carry-cot at the time. He slipped on a piece of rogue cucumber left over from an after-show party the night before in honour of Anita Harris' 10th year as Peter Pan. Bonnier flew up into the air and landed perfectly. It is never mentioned in her interviews because they fell out three years later when Vic wouldn't give her a second helping of lime jelly.

Victor and Barry believe the house to be haunted by the late great star of the music hall, Sir Harry Lauder. His presence appears (Dressed head to toe in tartan with his crooked stick) once aping on the strains and twice on a Saturday in the vestibule.

(handwritten annotations: Fred... mon... wha... meaning... (you...)

SCENE ONE

(EARLY IN THE MORNING. VICTOR AND BARRY'S TINY KITCHEN. BARRY IS STANDING CHOPPING PINEAPPLE, WHILST HUMMING "BALI HAI" FROM "SOUTH PACIFIC". VICTOR ENTERS CARRYING SOME RUSH MATTING, SOME CREPE PAPER AND A PAIR OF SCISSORS)

(handwritten: who's had a show last...)

BARRY:
Victor, have you got a list?

VICTOR:
No it's the lumps in the lino.

(THEY BOTH LAUGH)

VICTOR AND BARRY:
Oh dearie me!

BARRY:
No, but seriously, I mean have you got the breakfast checklist?

VICTOR:
No you've got it.

BARRY:
Have I?

(handwritten: night - down   alarm calls-k   on doors to start?)

VICTOR:
(PUTTING DOWN WHAT HE IS CARRYING)
Yes, there it is in your hand.

BARRY:
So it is. Oh I'm getting old, it's very worrying

VICTOR:
Why?

BARRY:
I keep forgetting things

VICTOR:
Oh

BARRY:
I'm getting old, it's very worrying

VICTOR:
Why?

BARRY:
I keep forgetting things.

VICTOR:
You've just said that

BARRY:
See what I mean!

VICTOR:
Butyou know, Baz, growing older affects us all in a multitude of unexpected and puzzling ways. Why only yesterday I clean forgot that Snickers was the new word for Marathon.

BARRY:
Oh that's a common mistake.

VICTOR:
That is as maybe, Barry, but it was very embarrassing at the time.

BARRY:
Oh I'm sure. I used to suffer that way. But now I don't let those marketing ploys get to me. Now I couldn't care a button or a fig for the everchanging trends in confectionary titles, and I've been that way ever since a banjo became a drifter.

VICTOR:
Have you?

BARRY:
Oh yes!

VICTOR:
You are an example to us all. Mushrooms?

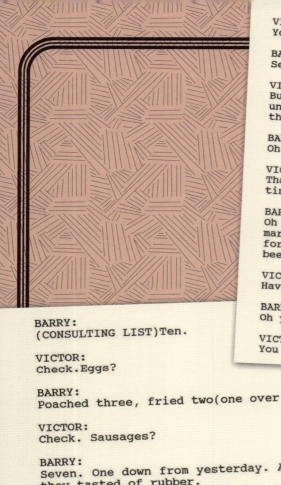

BARRY:
(CONSULTING LIST)Ten.

VICTOR:
Check.Eggs?

BARRY:
Poached three, fried two(one over easy) scrambled five.

VICTOR:
Check. Sausages?

BARRY:
Seven. One down from yesterday. And frankly I'm not surprised, they tasted of rubber.

VICTOR:
I forgot to tell you, one of my marigolds fell in the pan mid fry.

BARRY:
Victor! Right is that us then.

VICTOR:
Yes I think we are ready to ..beans!!!

(THERE IS A MAD FLURRY AS VICTOR AND BARRY DASH TO THE CUPBOARD, GET THE BEANS AND PUT THEM IN THE MICROWAVE)

VICTOR:
How many?

BARRY:
One two ....oh thirteen - full house of beans.

VICTOR:
Remind me to get some airwick solid for the hall.

BARRY:
Check

VICTOR:
So that's us then. How long till gong

BARRY:
Gong not long

VICTOR:
Long enough for a souchong?

BARRY:
You're not wrong

(THEY BOTH LAUGH)

V&B:
Oh dearie me

(THEY START TO MAKE A CUP OF TEA)

122

(ENTER VIOLA TUCK, VICTOR AND BARRY'S NEXT DOOR NEIGHBOUR WHO IS
A WAITRESS AND CLEANING LADY IN THEIR GUESTHOUSE)

VIOLA;
Morning Victor. Morning Barry.

VICTOR:
Morning Viola

BARRY:
How are you?

VIOLA:
Oh, don't ask. Terrible throbbing all night

BARRY:
That Spanish civil war wound acting up again?

VIOLA:
Aye. See me, see shrapnel? Riddled. If it wisnae for this
magnetic corset, I'd be a dead woman

VICTOR:
Carry on

VIOLA:
Well, the opposite polarities stop the bits of stray bullet from
moving and thereby entering my vital organs

BARRY:
Oh, it's amazing what they can do nowadays

VIOLA:
Aye, but it does have its drawbacks. I've been arrested twice for
settingoff the bleepers in C&A's , and there's nights when I
can't get a wink of sleep because it picks up Radio two Can you
imagine what it's like having Derek Jamieson emanating from your
mid-riff?

VICTOR:
Em, no. Oh Viola, you're such a poor wee scone (He cuddles her.)
Oh! Static!..Oh you wee Van der Graff! Now what's the theme of
today's breakfast?

BARRY:
The theme of today's breakfast is South Pacific. Have you got
your costume, Viola?

(VIOLA OPENS HER COAT TO REVEAL A GRASS SKIRT AND OTHER BITS OF
HAWAIIAN COSTUME.)

VIOLA:
I feel I'm being treated like a sex object.

BARRY:
You wish!

(VICTOR AND BARRY THROW OFF THEIR DRESSING GOWNS TO REVEAL
SAILORS OUTFITS)

V&B:
Gong time!

A CLOSE-UP OF A RATHER SHABBY GONG. WE HEAR VIC AND BAZ BU?
DON'T SEE THEM

VICTOR;
My turn

BARRY:
My turn

VICTOR:
My turn

BARRY:
My turn

(WE HEAR THE SOUND OF SOMEONE BEING SLAPPED. WE PULL BACK TO
REVEAL BARRY HOLDING THE STICK, AND VICTOR NEXT TO HIM WITH A
BRIGHT RED HANDMARK ON HIS FACE. BARRY GONGS THE GONG)

Marks and Spencers

Forbes Masson/Alan Cumming

Easy Listening Latin, ♩=82

Barry & Victor:

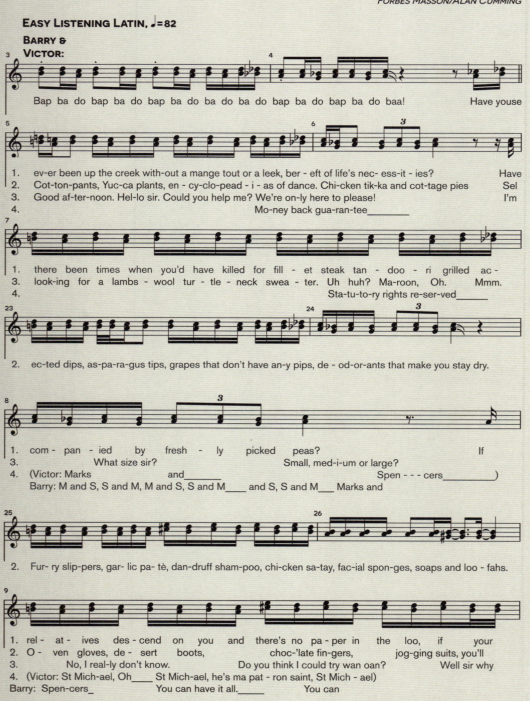

Bap ba do bap ba do bap ba do ba do ba do bap ba do bap ba do baa! Have youse

1. ev-er been up the creek with-out a mange tout or a leek, ber - eft of life's nec- ess-it - ies? Have
2. Cot-ton-pants, Yuc-ca plants, en - cy-clo-pead - i - as of dance. Chi-cken tik-ka and cot-tage pies Sel
3. Good af-ter-noon. Hel-lo sir. Could you help me? We're on-ly here to please! I'm
4. Mo-ney back gua-ran-tee_____

1. there been times when you'd have killed for fill - et steak tan - doo - ri grilled ac-
3. look-ing for a lambs - wool tur - tle - neck swea - ter. Uh huh? Ma-roon, Oh. Mmm.
4. Sta-tu-to-ry rights re-ser-ved_____

2. ec-ted dips, as-pa-ra-gus tips, grapes that don't have an-y pips, de - od-or-ants that make you stay dry.

1. com- pan - ied by fresh - ly picked peas? If
3. What size sir? Small, med-i-um or large?
4. (Victor: Marks and_____ Spen - - - cers_____)
Barry: M and S, S and M, M and S, S and M____ and S, S and M___ Marks and

2. Fur - ry slip-pers, gar- lic pa- tè, dan-druff sham-poo, chi-cken sa-tay, fac-ial spon-ges, soaps and loo - fahs.

1. rel - at - ives des - cend on you and there's no pa - per in the loo, if your
2. O- ven gloves, de - sert boots, choc-'late fin-gers, jog-ging suits, you'll
3. No, I real-ly don't know. Do you think I could try wan oan? Well sir why
4. (Victor: St Mich-ael, Oh____ St Mich-ael, he's ma pat - ron saint, St Mich - ael)
Barry: Spen-cers_ You can have it all._____ You can

Alan

Although slightly downhearted at the lack of enthusiasm for *V&B's B&B*, we were cheered when the legendary TV producer Beryl Vertue asked us to work on a new idea with her. Beryl had worked with the greats (Tony Hancock, Spike Milligan, Galton and Simpson) and was a producer on classic series such as *Steptoe and Son*, *Till Death Us Do Part*, *The Prime of Miss Jean Brodie*, all the way up to *Coupling* and *Sherlock* before her death in 2022.

With Beryl's encouragement and wisdom, we began to realise that for Victor and Barry to work in a sitcom format we needed to stick to our guns and take them back to their roots, both literally and figuratively. So they returned to the WRI Hall and The Kelvinside Young People's Amateur Dramatic Arts Society, and we let them be their real, authentic, theatrical selves. In the treatment, we purposely discussed the way that our performances had to be heightened. We even discussed how the colour palette needed to be vibrant in order to dispel any thoughts that this show was fixed in reality, as we'd been erroneously encouraged to do in our previous efforts.

Forbes

All their KYPADAS cohorts were back, more fully fleshed out as characters (with Lance Barclay staying Cockney as the token English person of the piece), as were some of our now apparently regular obsessions. That caravan in the back garden which had previously housed Brenda Turk (in *V&B's B&B*), as well as Barbara Windsor and Bonnie Langford (in the radio show *Come Away In*) would now host each episode's visiting celebrity guest who had begun their career under Victor and Barry's watchful

eye at KYPADAS (or not! See the Sheena Easton reference below…). Also, it seems we loved multiples: in *V&B's B&B* we had the Bunting triplets, here we have the Brodie quads: Betty, Mabel, Gwyneth and Sandra, the inhouse make-up artists.

Alan

However, just as we were beginning to make some headway with our latest Victor and Barry sitcom, we were asked by a script editor at the BBC to submit a non-Victor and Barry idea. That's actually what she said: 'Could you give us something that is not Victor and Barry?!'

Forbes

In 1993 we had a nibble. Around the late '80s/early '90s we spent a lot of time traveling up and down from Scotland to London, and so were regulars on both the British Midland and British Airways shuttle services. Eventually a lightbulb went on. We had always noticed the stewards onboard the flight and how theatrical they all were, with their routines for the safety demonstrations, their campery, their strictness, and their use of the little curtain at the end of the aisle.

Alan had the initial idea of setting something on a plane. The magazine onboard the British Airways flights is called *High Life*, and it seemed like a great title. We decided to have four regular characters instead of just us two. It would be Victor and Barry on a plane, but not Victor and Barry. Instead, they were Sebastian Flight (a play on the *Brideshead Revisited* character Sebastian Flyte) and Steve McCracken (I think there was a rude joke in there somewhere, Steve being a bit randy and desperate. Or maybe it was a John Byrne reference. In hindsight we missed a trick not calling him Steve McKeen).

Alongside us we thought there should be a crazy captain of the aircraft. We dreamt up Captain Duff. We also wanted a chief steward to be Steve and Sebastian's nemesis. A Scottish femme fatale. Shona seemed like a good Scots name. But what surname? A spurtle is a Scottish wooden kitchen implement for stirring porridge. It sounded good with Shona. It also sounded a bit rude. And so, Shona Spurtle was born. We wrote the ten-minute idea. The BBC liked it and commissioned a full script. The nibble had become a great big bite.

Alan

The script was commissioned under the auspices of a series called *Comic Asides*, essentially a set of pilots that might or might not go to series depending on the reaction they received. Looking back at it now, it was all very *Gladiator*. But we were victorious! Not only was our pilot script greenlit and then produced, but even before it was broadcast (in January 1994) we were commissioned to start writing a six-episode series.

Forbes

This was obviously all before the days of Zoom, so we actually had to travel to each other in order to write. Alan was living in London by now and I was still up in Glasgow. I remember one writing excursion where we met halfway and rented a cottage near Crewe to hole up for a few days and bash out some scripts. We went to a local pub to get drinks one night. I guess we must have looked like the rather flamboyant actory types we are, because the innkeeper eyed us with suspicion when we walked in and some of the regulars gave us odd looks. I went to the bar to buy some cigarettes (I sadly was still smoking at that point) and the unfriendly innkeeper replied, 'I don't think we have your sort of cigarettes here.'

On another writing session we stayed at the holiday home of John Ramage, brother of Gerry who directed *Laurel and Hardy*. John had played the dame in two of my pantos, and would go on to be the evil butcher McKinnon in my musical *Mince?* at Dundee Rep in 2001. He had a wee house in the south of France, near Toulouse, so Alan and I flew out there. Sometimes we wrote by the pool at the local lido. We had to be careful not to get our laptops covered in water from splashes.

With the script finally written, we needed to cast these characters. We saw some brilliant actors, and it was so interesting to be on the other side of the table in a casting room. The wonderful Siobhan Redmond walked in the room one afternoon and we knew immediately she was destined to be our Shona. Alan had seen Patrick Ryecart in a TV show and had mentioned him to me. He had said the immortal line, 'You smell like a brewery.' When I met Patrick, I knew that he was the right fit, too. Patrick is a genius and was so easy to write for, and also captured so much of Captain Duff's craziness. All four of us had such a ball working on the pilot, even though it was quite full-on for Alan and I.

Alan

If we couldn't get Victor and Barry their own sitcom, maybe we could take their energy and spirit and surreality and musicality and theatricality and aspirations and the peculiar antagonistic affection they had for each other, and make them flight attendants with big dreams? Not of putting on shows at the WRI Hall in Kelvinside, but of becoming the face of their airline's inflight video; or being promoted to the long-haul flights and their glamorous climes; or entering the Song for Europe contest?

And maybe it was for the best. Maybe Victor and Barry were never meant to have a sitcom. The theatre was in their blood, and the ephemeral, magical nature of it was always the medium for them. There are still many visual records of them around, from the huge amount of TV work we did, and it's always grand, unashamedly theatrical and uniquely them.

In a few pages is the opening scene of an early version of *The High Life* pilot script, complete with our notes and changes: many of the gags and routines were still gestating, Captain Duff is mentioned but doesn't appear in this version, and Air Scotia was Air Alba. But with its rhythms and its joy in language, it is surely the greatest Victor and Barry sitcom never made!

VICTOR & BARRY

PROPOSAL

This is a proposal for six half hour comedy programmes exploring the world of Kelvinside and its two leading light ent luminaries, Victor MacIlvaney and Barry McLeish, collectively known as Victor and Barry.

Each programme will have a self-contained storyline and will feature at least two songs written and performed by Victor and Barry, which are fully integrated into the action. It will feature other running characters, friends and aquaintances of Victor and Barry, who make up the Kelvinside Young People's Amateur Dramatic Art Society (K.Y.P.A.D.A.S) of which Victor and Barry are the founder members.

Victor and Barry are flatmates and live together at 22b Lacrosse Terrace. They live a strictly vegetarian lifestyle and drive a lead-free Hillman Imp. They have a regular column in the Kelvinside Recorder, 'Victor and Barry Speak Out'. They are K.Y.P.A.D.A.S' cultural ambassadors and their world-wide reputaion for excellence in amateur dramatics is known as far a field as Galashiels and Wick.

KELVINSIDE .... WHAT IS IT?

Kelvinside is a refined area of Glasgow, a cocoon from the outside world, a place where good manners and good elocution come before world problems,

> "The streets are so clean and the houses are so nice.
> It's very high in pollen and it's very low in vice."
> (West End Story)

It is a magical, mystical land where dreams can come true, filled with tea rooms, patisseries and gift shops, and definitely no chain stores or chip shops. There is an unspoken curfew at 10.25pm (after Sandy Gall's closing words), lights out by 10.30pm. The only person on the streets is the lonely figure of Doris Gloak, the bubbly divorcee, still searching for love.

The epicentre of Kelvinside life is the Women's Royal Institute Hall, home of the Kelvinside Young People's Amateur Dramatic Art Society. All cultural, social and emotional activities are played out there. Other venues for social gatherings include Ruari Blacklaws' butchers shop and Gloak's tea rooms.

STYLE

The moment the programme hits the screen, the audience enter the complete world of Kelvinside. Here all the characters are extraordinary and every aspect of their environment is odd. This effect is achieved firstly through the use of bright, vivid colours for the sets and the characters' costume and make-up, giving them an almost grotesque appearance.

~~Secondly,~~ all the performances are very theatrical. Not only are they bigger than you would normally expect to see on television, but the action is staged and played out at a relentless pace. The performances are camp and tacky but they are also meticulous and skillful.

Lastly, the dialogue reinforces this heightened naturalism. All the characters use extreme language, particularly when describing mundanities. People have 'speeches' through which they reveal something about themselves using unconventional language. No-one ever abbreviates or interrupts, 'speeches' are always allowed to run their full dramatic course. There is no wasted dialogue, everything either moves the plot forward or enhances character development. The dialogue is very dense, as Victor and Barry would say,

"It's very rich, we're not talking a finger buffet here,
we're talking banquet. A televisual three-course meal,
inclusive of tea, toast, tip and complimentary post purvey polo".

MUSIC

There will be two musical numbers in each episode, sung mainly by Victor and Barry, though they will include other characters. The songs have a classic 'Hollywood' feel to them and will be performed in a very dramatic, over-the-top way. Singing has the same effect on the characters of Kelvinside, as it does in Hollywood movies, it is a way of dealing with problems and unhappiness, and generally makes everyone feel much better about their lives.

Much of the action takes place in Victor and Barry's home where every crisis is dealt with as if it had global implications. People regularly call on Victor and Barry at home to ask advice and to plead for particular roles in the Society's up and coming theatrical productions.

The heart of Kelvinside life and social activity is of course the Women's Royal Institute Hall, home of K.Y.P.A.D.A.S. All human life and emotions are played out there: people argue, form alliances and plot against each other, it is a place where people fulfil their fantasies.

In Victor and Barry's back garden they keep a caravan which houses the week's celebrity guest, supposedly. These celebrities are people who began their careers with Victor and Barry at K.Y.P.A.D.A.S and went on to greater things. Victor and Barry allow their caravan to be used as a retreat from the harsh, cruel world of showbusiness. They provide the celebrity guest with the opportunity to seek advice and guidance from their artistic gurus.

The celebrity is only allowed into the house to use the bathroom and to make the occasional telephone call (on the guests payphone) to their agent. Victor and Barry find their guests very tiresome, though they always find time to sit down with them and tell them just exactly where they went wrong with their careers.

There will be times when the audience never sees the supposed celebrity guest eg: Sheena Easton locks herself in the downstairs toilet and cries throughout an entire episode because Prince has chucked her.

VIOLA TUCK is Victor and Barry's next door neighbour and their closest friend.

~~She is 60 years old and has the appearance of a gentle "wee wifey". She is willingly dominated by Victor and Barry who she worships.~~ They never allow her to appear on stage though it is her greatest ambition to do so. She is the props girl for the K.Y.P.A.D.A.S., and she can often be found backstage sobbing behind her props desk.

Viola is member of the Communist Party and runs the local 'Good as New Shop'. ~~Victor and Barry regularly see streams of young radicals leaving her house.~~ As Victor remarks,

"Viola's body is littered with shrapnel she received during the Spanish Civil War. She can pick up Radio Moscow if she sits with her legs in the air".

DORIS GLOAK is Kelvinside's "bubbly divorcee". ~~She is a very attractive~~

Doris runs the local tea rooms, 'Gloaks', and loves playing the hostess. She has no children, her husband ran off with a young waitress ten years ago. ~~As a~~

The night Doris' husband ran off with the waitress was the last night she performed as the Society's Grand Dame. The shock made her lose her voice and she now mimes in the chorus. ~~So in addition to losing her husband she~~ ~~her place in the So~~

Doris shows her admiration for Victor and Barry by naming Gloaks' fruit cocktails after K.Y.P.A.D.A.S. hit musicals, eg 'The Bald! Breaker', 'Gordon Jackson Superstar Slammer' and 'Ryvita Marguerita'.

RENEE ROBERTS is the Grand Dame of K.Y.P.A.D.A.S. A very glamorous woman in her late 50's whose pretensions are on a par with Victor and Barry's. She is a widow and makes her living taking in pupils and passing on her theatrical skills.

Renee has a string of toyboys who she refers to as her "pupils". These Adonis figures never speak but she usually has one of them in tow.

Renee's heroines are Barbra Streisand and Barbara Dickson.

LANCE BARCLAY is Kelvinside's local plumber and joiner, he is also the Society's choreographer. Lance is a straight-talking cockney, not a man to mince his words or beat about the bush. He can usually be seen in his filthy overalls attending to someone's septic tank or with his head under the sink.

In the evenings, Lance can be found in a pair of tights leading the warm-up session before rehearsals, this is when he truly comes into his own.

GWYNETH AND SANDRA are two of the Brodie quads, sisters to Betty and Mabel. They are self employed Mobile Make Up Demonstrators, they are also K.Y.P.A.D.A.S. make up girls.

They ~~are very busy women and are always trying to get "pally"~~ with Victor and ~~Barry~~. They are always together and look identical in their gingham dresses and National Health glasses. There are times when they speak in unison and the only way to tell them apart is to remember that Sandra has a plaster over the right lens of her glasses, and Gwyneth has a plaster over the left.

y's attention. They regularly send "love tokens" to Victor and Barry, including a brick wrapped in a love letter through their window.

BRENDA TURK is a Romany and mystic extraordinaire. She is a great friend of Victor and Barry's who regularly reads their tea leaves and gives them spiritual guidance on important matters. She makes her living using her psychic powers to play the stock market and to bet on horses and dogs. Brenda is also a great advocate of urinology.

131

PRODUCTIONS STAGED BY THE KELVINSIDE YOUNG PEOPLE'S AMATEUR DRAMATIC ART SOCIETY

The Boyfriend -   The first ground breaking musical staged by the Society.

Call Me Madam -   Tragedy struck this production when Renee Roberts was involved in a trolley collision in Safeway on opening night. She was supposed to be playing the lead role of 'the Madam'. Ophelia Wishart had to stand in, miming the words, as Barry sang and spoke from the wings.

A SERIES OF WESTERN MUSICALS

Oh! The Grosvenor -   Adapted from Oklahoma! and set in a wild hotel

Paint Your Volkswagen -   Set in a garage.

Seven Bridies for Seven Brothers -   Pastie fights and fratricide in this rip roarin' humdinger of a show, set in Tunnocks Bakery.

West End Story -   Gangland warfare meets Romeo and Juliet but not nearly as harsh as the Bernstein. As opposed to the Jets and the Sharks, the Turbos and the Trouts, Barry played Duane Turbo and Victor played Ricardo Trout. They felt the name Maria was a bit religious (especially for Glasgow) so they changed it to Sigourney.

MUSICALS THAT WERE STOLEN BY 'SOMEONE ELSE'

Victor And His Amazing Multi-Textured Cardigan - A semi-agnostic musical.

Gordon Jackson Superstar!

Ryvita -   A musical about a revolutionary South American dietician.

Cuts -   Based on Luigi McLeishe's poems which had the whole company dressed as ferrets, acting out the affects of the Thatcher years on Social Service expenditure.

HORROR MUSICALS INSPIRED BY THE RSC's CARRIE

Trout -   Based on the film 'Jaws', in which a killer trout terrorizes paddlers in the River Kelvin. Special effects included a large water tank for an under-water ballet. Unfortunately, Ophelia Wishart who was playing the lead role of the trout, dived too deep and got the bends.

The Excorcist -   Chirpy musical based on satanic possession. Featured the hit song "Your Granny Sucks Eggs in Helensburgh".

Creme Passionelle -   Agatha Christie murder mystery musical about home baking.

AVANTE GARDI MUSICALS

Bald! -   Sexual politics with a small 'p', introduced body stockings to Kelvinside.

"Young, free and careless, I'm utterly hairless,
Bald! Bald!
I'm not hirsute, I'm as bald as a coot,
Bald! Bald!
No more dandruff, no more lice, I think being bald is nice,
Bald! Bald!

THE HIGH LIFE

BY ALAN CUMMING AND FORBES MASSON

scene one

Steve is in the locker room of AIR ALBA airlines. He
is at his locker, changing into his uniform. On his
locker door he has pictures of various stars...Bette
Davis, Judy Garland, and a signed photo of Alan
Titchmarsh. He is wearing a walkman and listening to
The Pet Shop Boys greatest hits, and singing along.

STEVE:

(SINGS) Che Guevara and Debussy to a disco beat...

ENTER SEBASTIAN DRESSED IN A RAIN SOAKED MACKINTOSH.

SEBASTIAN

~~Hiya Steve~~ Just shut it, Steve

STEVE:
God ~~Almighty~~,
Oh ~~hiya~~ Sebastian! You ~~caught me~~! What kept you ~~this morning~~?
Forget to wind up snoopy again.

SEBASTIAN

said
1] ~~Shut~~ it, crusty gusset
Snoopy barked on cue at 5.45. There wis a pile up on
the slip road. Detour via Dalmarnock, then I
recollected that I'd neglected ma gel sap, so it wis a
u-turn home. Back at the ranch cannae find ruddy sap,
so resort to mousse. Applying mousse when I spys gel
sap out of the corner of my eye, bunged behind the
Johnsons..

SEBASTIAN
~~Lotion~~ Total rinse in order. Plus application of said
sap. Hence the delay...see mondays....PISH! Pass ma
slacks.

STEVE:
~~Can do~~. Oh oh. ~~In need of an iron.~~ You'll be needing your steam smoother

SEBASTIAN
~~Ach they'll~~ do. Am I ever without it (Proceeds to steam his trousers)
What time's take off?

STEVE:

Five after seven.

SEBASTIAN

Crickey!

SEBASTIAN

How?

STEVE: ~~first~~ Snr

Wis up ~~at Saturday~~ wi ma stomach.   romantic disaster

SEBASTIAN

How?

STEVE: with Rhonda McAllison

Dubious Dansak and corked Blue Nun ∧ at the Shish Mahal.

~~plink~~ ~~for a~~

STEVE:

Uh huh. Better get a jildy oan. You for coffee.

SEBASTIAN   Cook, Steve. How many times...

Caffiene gives me gas. Mash me a peppermint.

STEVE:

~~Sorry~~ We're fresh out or pepper~~~ ~~can do!~~ Bicky?

STEVE:

Well I wis thinking oan ma feet!

SEBASTIAN

Weekend good to you?

STEVE:

Hardly

SEBASTIAN

Nippy bum?

STEVE:

Inferno! So I hardly need to tell you that the planned

SEBASTIAN

wi ma love handles? Nut. ~~Who're ue oan wi?~~ Check the   just the on
                                            Seb: Well maybe. Seb: ~~love~~ ↑ Cae
~~rota, chum.~~   (look) ↗   Steve Chocolate   ~~to the~~ ↑ the
                  Steve: Aye, right enough. ~~Doyou want to know~~   po

STEVE:

Uh huh. Pilot's Duff. Co-pilot's MacIsaac.

Purser's...oh fiddle..it's fraulien SS

SEBASTIAN

Oh France no her. No Shona Spurtle.

STEVE: looking for

HM HM And she's been in ~~after~~ you. So if she asks you

were under the doctor with your verukas.

SEBASTIAN

VERUKAS!

post-meal intimacy, he said
raving with Rhonda ~~~~~~~ S: How? I went down the cludgie... 'Lassie.'
    S: Well, I ~~~~~~ she's a nice lassie I don't think she'd have
                                    appreciated me chucking
~~~~~~~~~~ taste of fish.   Liz and Richard went for a burton. These   up mid snog.
                            Aye ~~~~~~~~~ have ~~~~~~~~
× ~~~~~~~~   Aye which that great croupier in
                                the sky was dishing out the love chips,
                                    your ~~~~ cards were marked   come up, did it?
        SEBASTIAN   S: Eh S: You're not what you'd call successful in the
                                                        to snagging game
        Still feeling dicky in the lumber region then?   S: I have my moments
                                                    S: Aye, few and far between.
                                                    Mind you, there's
STEVE: Now I know how the pope felt. And   nothin' wrong with
                                                    being celibate. Look
        Affirmative. The thought of dishing out hot full   what it's done for Cliff Richard's
        englishes to a clutch of halitosis ridden pinstripes   skin

        is creating ructions in ma colon as we speak. So all

        in all. saturday wis a.... wis a..

SEBASTIAN

Whit?..

STEVE:

a.. saturday wis a.. oh ..a..

SEBASTIAN

Whit...a washout?

STEVE:

No! A..a..

SEBASTIAN

Whit..awry..agog..around..about..agogo..aghast...accapella
...accapulco...whit?!

        STEVE:

        Saturday wis a....

        STEVE:&SEBASTIAN

        SHITE NIGHT!   .

Alan
And here is the first draft of the safety information
announcement...

SEB
Ladies and Gentlemen, please listen carefully
to this important safety information,
demonstrated for youse today by our
two lovely redheads, Steve and Shona.
Can you guess which one of them gets their
red hair out of a bottle? Clue. It's
the one with the baggy chin, the
dropping chest and the several
shades too dark foundation. That's
right, it's Shona the new face of
Air Scotia. Hard to believe, eh?
I was up for that. Didn't get it.
But I'm not bitter. Not.
But back to safety.
(VERY FAST) Emergency exits are
here, here and here. Oh, I'll say
that again. Here, here and here.
If we crash, the aisle'll be lit
up like Blackpool. It'll be lovely
with fairy lights in the dark.
Twinkle, Twinkle. If you canny
breathe, some masks will appear.
Put them on like this and gie them
a good tug. You'll be usedto that,
Shona.
Now, life jackets. Very useful
in water, but not very effective
if we crash land on concrete, which
let's face it, is much more likely.
Put it over your head like this,
wrap the straps like this, tie it
like this. Inflate it like this...

My, Shona! You do that
awfy well!

135

1994

SITCOM SCIENCE FONT FARCE GORDON'S GRIN SALMONY SWAN-SONG

Alan

For the first few months of the year, I was back at the Donmar playing the Emcee in *Cabaret* (and as I mentioned earlier, stealing some of Victor and Barry's material!). Forbes would follow me into that same theatre as after my run ended, he opened in Simon Donald's brilliant play *The Life of Stuff*, originally produced up in Edinburgh at the Traverse.

We were also busy getting *The High Life* scripts finished. Forbes would occasionally come down to London and we would have manic writing sessions together. I was going through a pretty turbulent period in my personal life at the time, so those days with him laughing and acting out the nascent characters and escapades of Steve and Sebastian were bright lights on quite a gloomy horizon. I suppose it was also another example of the dark, dark humour we so love in Scotland. You have to laugh or you'd greet is how the saying goes, and that is exactly what I was doing in those writing sessions with him at the time.

But it wasn't all fun and japes...

Forbes

We were assigned a script editor who really didn't understand us. They gave us a little pamphlet entitled 'how to write a sitcom' which had simplistic 'scientific formulas' on how to produce the best sitcom. 'If one character is tidy, the other should be messy' etc. It would have been laughable, except for the fact that a sitcom written this way wouldn't have been. If you see what I mean.

We kept saying, look, we have created the characters, we have performed characters like them on the coalface, in the raw, in front of audiences; we have honed this act for years and we know what works for us. Our style of comedy is bizarre and unique, but it works. It was another case of 'You boys don't understand television.' They also didn't like the fact we both said 'Oh dearie me' at the same time. They said that no one ever speaks at the same time in a sitcom! We just ignored them. Ironically, this would become our most quoted line from the series...

Alan

We delivered one episode, the sort of *Batman*-style one where Steve and Sebastian find a floppy disk a passenger has left in their seatback pocket; little do they know that it contains the ideal ratio of condensed milk and sugar to make the perfect tablet, and that it's been stolen by an evil biscuit magnate named Vincent Stoat. In a script meeting, the head of comedy told us that this was a second-series episode. The way we felt at the time there was no chance of there ever being a second series, so at the next meeting we told them we had made some changes based on their ideas

and handed the exact same script back in again, but in a different font. The word came back from on high that they felt we had addressed all their worries and we got a green light for the episode. They obviously hadn't even read the 'new' version because not one single word of it had changed! It's difficult to listen to or respect people when they are so blatantly lazy about their jobs.

Forbes

There was another episode where Air Scotia was hosting a Saga tour, and naturally Steve and Sebastian asked the passengers to remove their false teeth as there was going to be some turbulence. They deposited said gnashers in a bucket in the onboard fridge. Alas the fridge was faulty so when they go to return the teeth to their passengers, they discover the teeth are frozen and put them in the microwave to defrost them. They then deliver rather warm, steaming teeth to the passengers while saying 'hot teeth sir, madam', mimicking the way stewards offer hot towels.

The script editor strongly queried this and said somewhat snootily, referring to the handbook, 'This wouldn't happen on a plane.' Of course it wouldn't, we said. IT. WAS. A. COMEDY. NOT. A. DOCUMENTARY. We had reached the point where it was becoming impossible and something had to give. We parted company with the script editor and were left to our own devices.

Alan

The casting of that particular scene was hysterical. I remember being in a casting suite at the Beeb with various elderly actors and we had to ask them to take their teeth out. We felt so embarrassed to be asking them to do it. One old gent said, 'I think there has been some mistake. My agent may have told you I have false teeth, but they won't come out. They're implants!' We eventually had the legendary John Grieve come in, who withdrew his teeth with aplomb and then slipped them back into his mouth as if they were hot and said, 'Ooh! Burny, burny!' He completely understood the gag. What a joy it was to work with him.

Talking of legends, we also got to work with Molly Weir, who improvised during the filming of one scene in the last (extremely surreal) episode. At one point she started singing 'A Gordon for Me'. We kept it in.

BBC TV presents

The team that brought you "VICTOR & BARRY"
in

"THE HIGH LIFE"

A new comedy for BBC2
written by & starring

ALAN CUMMING & FORBES MASSON
with
Siobhán Redmond & Patrick Ryecart

Recording at BBC Television Centre on Wednesday evening
19, 26 October, 2, 9 16 & 23 November 1994

For FREE tickets please apply in writing with an SAE
stating show, number of tickets required
and daytime telephone number to:

THE BBC TICKET UNIT, ROOM 301
DESIGN BUILDING, TELEVISION CENTRE
WOOD LANE, LONDON W12 7RJ

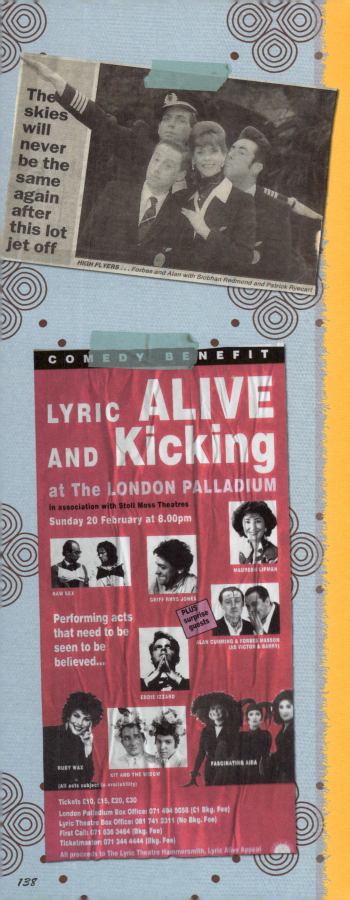

The skies will never be the same again after this lot jet off

HIGH FLYERS . . . Forbes and Alan with Siobhan Redmond and Patrick Ryecart

COMEDY BENEFIT

LYRIC ALIVE AND Kicking

at The LONDON PALLADIUM

in association with Stoll Moss Theatres

Sunday 20 February at 8.00pm

RAW SEX

GRIFF RHYS JONES

MAUREEN LIPMAN

Performing acts that need to be seen to be believed...

PLUS surprise guests

ALAN CUMMING & FORBES MASSON (AS VICTOR & BARRY)

EDDIE IZZARD

RUBY WAX

KIT AND THE WIDOW

FASCINATING AIDA

(All acts subject to availability)

Tickets £10, £15, £20, £30
London Palladium Box Office: 071 494 5056 (£1 Bkg. Fee)
Lyric Theatre Box Office: 081 741 2311 (No Bkg. Fee)
First Call: 071 836 3464 (Bkg. Fee)
Ticketmaster: 071 344 4444 (Bkg. Fee)
All proceeds to The Lyric Theatre Hammersmith, Lyric Alive Appeal

Forbes

We probably got away with so much Scottish rudeness because the series was made by BBC London. Phrases like 'shut yer fud!' and 'fuddy hell' probably sound innocuous south of Gretna Green. However, sometimes the lack of understanding was a problem. There was a particularly funny moment when props arrived with the food for a scene which we had described as needing not a full English, but a full Scottish breakfast. In the script, we said that it should be sliced sausage on the plate. We as Scots know that sliced sausage (or Lorne sausage as it's called in Glasgow) is square but what turned up was a link sausage sliced lengthways. Sausagey Sassenachs!

Alan

There was one bonus. Fortunately, we were assigned a BBC director called Angie De Chastelai Smith, who completely understood us and did a fantastic job on the series. Her partner John Record was D.O.P. and he shot it beautifully. We are all still very close friends.

We wrote and recorded the theme tune, which was based around the 'High Caledonia!' song from *Clean Ripe Gentlemen*, and shot an extraordinary dance sequence in a hangar at Prestwick Airport choreographed by Hot Gossip's Carol Fletcher. At one point we were being filmed together singing to a moving camera for the closing titles. We kept moving and going out of focus. Eventually, they basically put a rope around us and tied it to the camera to keep us at the right distance.

Forbes

We got to work with some of the greats we had met and worked with in Scottish theatre: Bob Carr, Jenny McCrindle, Ronnie Letham, Alex Norton, Gerda Stevenson and John Ramage.

Many scenes, including the plane aisle ones were filmed in Scotland, but the main studio scenes were shot live, in front of an audience at the old BBC TV Centre in White City, London. It was such a thrill to be working in that iconic building. You had to sign in at the desk in front of security guards. I remember going in one day and the guard asked for my name. I said, 'Forbes Masson'. The guard looked at his list and said 'No, we don't have you down. We have Four Masons.' After some persuading and a few phone calls, he let me in.

Each episode rehearsed for a week in BBC rooms in Acton Town. On one occasion we got in the lift there along with Rik Mayall and Ade Edmondson, who were rehearsing *Bottom*. Alan had worked with Rik, and was chatting to him, but I went a bit weak at the knees as I was a massive fan.

Alan

The first episode was broadcast on January 6th 1995, and it was a bit of a sensation. I don't think people had ever seen anything like it on BBC2. In the UK it is still, to this day, out of all the things I've done in my career, the show that most people stop me about in the street. 'Oh dearie me' is still regularly shouted at us both! One of the downsides, though, was every time we got on a plane for many years afterwards, as we approached the staff welcoming passengers at the end of the jetway, we would be called 'fat bum' or 'sweaty', just as we had done to the TV passengers in the show!

Forbes

On one flight, the air stewards danced up the aisle, kicking their legs while singing the theme tune. I remember a slightly odd moment when one steward said to me, 'I love *The High Life*! It's so much like real life!' Our ex-script editor would have been be so pleased…

Siobhan, Patrick, Alan and I had such a crazy time working on the show. I think its humour and wit still stand up. It means so much that people continue to remember it fondly, and it was such an honour that one of the episodes was picked to be screened as part of the BBC's centenary celebrations.

I really wanted to do more episodes and I was terribly sad we didn't. But by that point, our lives and careers were quickly going in completely different directions. In hindsight, like with Victor and Barry, leaving people wanting more was probably the right decision.

Alan

The no-more-episodes thing was my doing. I said no. But I agree with Forbes; it is really lovely that both V&B and *The High Life*, though finite and relatively brief, have such a special place in people's hearts.

Early in 1994, I was asked to perform at a benefit for The Lyric, which was in real financial trouble at the time. A couple of years before, I had done the UK premiere there of David Hirson's amazing play *La Bête*, so they reached out to me. I almost respectfully declined because at the time I was terrified at the thought of going on stage and performing as me! I didn't have a solo act, but I *did* have a double act. We both knew that Victor and Barry would give their teeth (all of them) to perform at The London

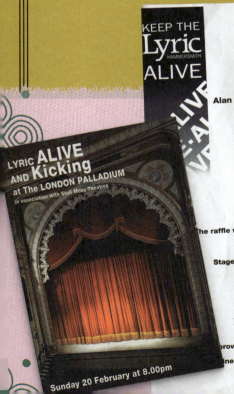

KEEP THE
Lyric
HAMMERSMITH
ALIVE

LYRIC A...
AND Ki...
at The LO...
in association w...

Alan Cumming & Forbes Masson
(as Victor and Barry)
Fascinating Aida
Stephen Fry
Eddie Izzard
Kit and The Widow
Maureen Lipman
Raw Sex
Griff Rhys Jones
Ruby Wax

Plus surprise guests

There will be one interval.
The raffle will be drawn on stage after the interval

Director	Peter James
Producer	Clare Fox
Stage Management	Nicole Griffiths
	Marian Spon
	Zoe Gould
	Helen Wilding
	John Power
Sound	Gary Giles
Lighting	Mick Hughes

PRODUCTION CREDITS:
Thanks to:
Piano by **Markson Pianos**
providing the spring water and water cooler
Telephone - 071 231 7724
ine Coffee Limited – Telephone: 0923 2101
Kirstie Smith
Jennifer Spence
British Midland Airways

LYRIC **ALIVE**
AND **Kicking**
at The LONDON PALLADIUM
in association with Stoll Moss Theatres

Sunday 20 February at 8.00pm

Alan Cumming

Trained: Royal Scottish Academy of Music and Drama.

Theatre: includes the title role in *Hamlet* (English Touring Theatre tour/Donmar Warehouse – Shakespeare Globe Award nomination). *La Bete* (Lyric Hammersmith – Olivier Award nomination), *The Conquest of the South Pole* (Traverse/Royal Court – Olivier Award nomination). Also seasons at the Tron, Glasgow; Royal Lyceum, Edinburgh; Dundee Rep; Bristol Old Vic; Musselburgh; anc tours with Borderline, Theatre Workshop and Glasgow Citizens' TAG.

RNT: *Accidental Death of an Anarchist* (Comedy Performance of the Year, Olivier Award 1991), *Romeo and Juliet* (RNT studio). RSC: *As you Like It*, Singer.

He is currently starring in *Cabaret* at the Donmar Warehouse.

Television: most recently *The High Life, Mickey Love, A Word in Your Era, The Story of Frankenstein, The Last Romantics, Dread Poets' Society, Bernard and the Genie* (Top Television Newcomer, British Comedy Award 1992).

Film: *Passing Glory, Prague* (Best Actor, Atlantic Film Festival 1992. Scottish BAFTA Best Film Actor nomination), *Second Best, The Clinch, That Sunday*.

Radio: *1066 and All That, Morning Story, Keats: Letters from Burns Country, The Prisoners of Penicuik,* and *Melville Bay*.

Writing: co-adapted *Accidental Death of an Anarchist* and *Dragon* for the RNT. Co-wrote and performed with Forbes Masson several Victor and Barry shows including *In the Scud* (Assembly Rooms, Edinburgh/Purcell Rooms) and *See Victor and Barry and Faint* (Assembly Rooms, Edinburgh/Donmar Warehouse/Sydney Opera House and Australian tour). They also wrote *Babes in the Wood* (Tron, Glasgow) and a series for BBC 2, *The High Life.* Alan has also written a short film, *Butter*.

Directing: *Bonjour La, Bonjour* by Michel Tremblay at the RNT studio.

Forbes Masson

Trained: Royal Scottish Academy of Music and Drama.

Theatre includes: Pasha in *Cinzano, The Real World,* Buttons/Troon Colquoon in *Cinderella* (Tron, Glasgow), Alec/Header in *Gamblers* (Tron/Traverse co-production), *Clocked Out* and *Loose Ends* (Traverse, Edinburgh), *Great Expectations* (TAG Theatre, Scottish tour), *Victor & Barry* (Edinburgh Festival/Donmar Warehouse and tour of Australia including Sydney Opera House and tour of *The Lady in the Dark* (Scottish Opera – Edinburgh Festival), Aiden Quinn in *Elizabeth Gordon Quinn* (Traverse, Mayfest, Scottish tour and London Fringe), Stan Laurel in *Laurel and Hardy* (Edinburgh Festival/Wellington Festival, New Zealand), *Me Myself Us* (Mayfest, Glasgow & Edinburgh Festival), *Lust* by Iain Heggie (Mayfest, Edinburgh Festival) and most recently *The Life of Stuff* at the Donmar Warehouse.

Television includes: *Taggart* (and many others for Scottish Television), *My Dead Dad and Dad on Arrival* (STV), *City Lights* (BBC 1), *Loose Ends* (BBC Scotland), *Red Dwarf* (BBC 2) and *The High Life* (BBC 2) among others.

Writing credits include: *Jack and the Beanstalk* (1991) and *Cinderella* (Tron Glasgow 1992/ Royal Lyceum Edinburgh 1993), *Snow White* (1993) (Tron, Glasgow) and *The High Life* (BBC 2 sitcom).

Film: *Loser's Blues.*

Radio includes: *Speak To Us Ruth; The Boy Who Wanted Peace; The Hitler Diaries; Dirty Dustbin And The Binblaster; Loose Ends; A Halloween Tale; The Last Of These; Water, Water, Everywhere; The Kingdom of the Wind; Men of the Charlie; Hair in the Gate; Forbes Masson Half Hour; Weir of Hermiston; The Wrong Box* (all BBC).

Palladium, where the benefit was taking place, so I suggested to Forbes that we do the show together and make this V&B's final performance. What better way to go out?

We thought it would be perfect to do a condensed version of *In the Scud*, which ended, of course, with Victor and Barry literally dying. At one point in the show, Victor and Barry decide to stop for a snack and open a flask of salmon soup. Brenda Turk, their mystic friend, had called them onstage earlier saying she had had a premonition of doom and that two names were coming through: Ella and Sam… Victor and Barry thought she was raving but just as they are about to close the evening…

Forbes

It was such a buzz to be on that stage, with all its showbiz history. We went down an absolute storm, closing the set with 'Most Dramatic Way.' As we sang the last few notes, we looked at each other, knowing it would be the last time Victor and Barry would ever perform together. But how higher could they go than playing The London Palladium? And then, as I played the final chord, I slumped onto the piano as if Victor had died; at the exact same time, Alan slumped onto the piano too. And that was it. RIP V&B. The place went nuts. It was such a blast, but it was best to leave on a high.

Many's the time we've said, we'd forego our
 daily bread
Just so we could hit the heights before we wound
 up dead
We've gurned, we've sniffed, we've cried, taken
 the hump, much more besides
So that we can guarantee our own way's
 not denied
If despair is rife, youse have got to live your
 life
In a most dramatic way, in a most dramatic way
Youse only have one chance, so grab it with both
 your hands
Try not to step on others' toes in life's multi-
coloured dance
Be strong, be firm, be loud; never be drab, never
 be dowdy
Wear a silk cravat and then you'll stand out
 from the crowd
Shout 'luvvie' and 'hello darling', tell the
 papers lies
Drink gallons, be rude in restaurants and always
 patronise
Have saunas and lots of massages, laugh loudly and
 annoy the passengers when you're on the bus
Be jooshy, date a floozy, put a bit about

Be gallus, emulate Dallas, throw the rule book
 out. Laugh your dentures out!
If life hurts you to the marrow, you can't thole
 all those slings and arrows
Don't procrastinate. Act now it's not too late
 Dive in, the water's great

(Spoken)
V: All the world's a stage, some of us are
 players, others merely spectate
B: Don't sit in the stalls forever, get up and
 do your turn
V: Before the walkdown starts and you're not in
 it
B: That velvet curtain soon must drop
V: Don't just think about it
B: No more rehearsals
V&B: It's showtime!
If despair is rife, youse have got to live your
 life in a most dramatic way, in a most dramatic
 way, in a most dramatic way!

END

Forbes

So that is it. The Victor and Barry Years. It's been an extraordinary thing to meander down memory close. Extraordinary, because I still can't quite get over our energy, fearlessness and chutzpah, to come up with these silly characters that took on a life of their own.

Alan

It has been incredible to look back at it all and realise that Victor and Barry were a kind of Scottish alternative to the alternative comedy of the '80s. Alternative comedy was a reaction to the sexist and racist material prevalent in mainstream clubs and TV at the time and was usually served up with a liberal peppering of political ranting. Though Victor and Barry engaged in politics with opening gambits such as *Kelvinside is a city in Glasgow, Glasgow is a city in Scotland, and Scotland is a country to the north of England and to the left of Mrs Thatcher*, and eulogising their beloved home in the song, 'Kelvinside Men' thus: *Some people would move away if they had to pay the kind of poll-tax we don't pay*, sung as they set fire to a poll tax form in the song's video no less! – ranters they were not.

And although ever the optimists, they did not flinch from embracing the less attractive sides of life in their beloved Glasgow – *It's a town with guts, you see some on the pavement. The people have names like Senga, Shug and Lloyd. Some of them aren't quite the full shilling. You'd be the same if you were unemployed.* But mostly Victor and Barry sang songs about how good things used to be, not how bad they currently were. The struggle to fit all the shopping in the boot of the Hillman Imp was the struggle of their proletariat, the convenience of Marks and Spencers' ready to eat meals more pressing than the philosophies of that other Marx.

Forbes

And oh my, how time flies! We were both so young, so much part of each other's lives, we did so much in such a short space of time and we were virtually in each other's pockets (as Alan has said, 'being in a double act is like being married without the sex.') so I suppose it was sadly inevitable that after the whirlwind career of Victor and Barry and their alter egos in *The High Life*, we both had to fly the nest, to be able push ourselves, to grow and explore other areas of our lives and careers. As an artist it's important to never feel safe, no matter how scary insecurity is. To keep growing artistically, you must constantly challenge yourself and take risks. The experience of working with Alan, building our creative confidence together, learning so much from each other – Alan's drive and self-assurance still are inspirational to me – show that Victor and Barry were the building blocks for the success of both our careers. If I hadn't done Victor and Barry, I wouldn't have had the courage to write my own work, like the big Scottish musical *STIFF!* I created in 1999.

I wouldn't have met Michael Boyd and go with him to work on so many productions at the RSC.

I wouldn't have realised my childhood dream of becoming an actor.

Alan

I agree. Victor and Barry taught me so much about being open as a performer. Shakespeare soliloquies are basically stand up comedy routines (often without the jokes!) and so I don't think I would have been the Hamlet I was without V&B's influence.

Also we had balls of fucking steel. We would walk on stage and literally not know how the show was going to end. I sometime started playing a song at the piano unsure if I knew all the chords! On stage, with real people who had paid money to see us! But we got away with it. Or rather, we made our mistakes and our lacks into a virtue and a positive, and actually who doesn't love when performers screw things up or forget their lines? Very early on we both stumbled on that realisation and milked it.

To this day, when I am singing in a concert, if I make a mistake or don't feel happy with the way a song is going, I'll stop and start it again, and that nerve, that cocky vulnerability is all because of Vic and Baz, and Forbes and me.

Forbes

Looking back, what is a common theme, is the fight we both had to face against that negative, *oh you can't do that, you're not good enough* voice. From my careers advisor at school, who 'advised' me not to be an actor, to the doubting people we met throughout those years. Fighting them, finding the confidence to just dream, believe and create and the power that gives you, to be independent, is truly transformative. I look at our trajectory and see it mirroring the fate of our dear country itself. I hope that reading this book will encourage others to dream, believe and create. Confidence is all you need. It's what I tell my kids. Dreams can come true, but it's all up to you, in the end.

Alan

Getting older means you can look back and see the bigger picture. There was a time in the '90s when we had no contact for several years, and it was very, very difficult for me. Memory is collective and so without access to the person who I loved so much and had gone through so much with, I felt a whole swathe of my life was suddenly inaccessible, almost as if it hadn't even happened. The fact that this coincided with a divorce and my moving to a new country made it seem doubly, or triply intense. Out of the blue on Hogmanay 1998, Forbes called me in New York City, and I couldn't have wished for a better start to the new year. There have been some bumps in the road, but we have been in each other's lives ever since, and doing this book has brought us closer and made us stronger than ever.

Forbes

Alan is right. The looking back brings the blurry past into focus. I went through a very dark patch in the mid '90s, when I lost both my parents within six months of each other, and it took me a long time on my own, licking my wounds, to recover. I felt lost, trying to cope. It felt like everything around me had collapsed. I found it difficult to keep going. But keeping going is the secret. Time truly does heal.

It's been a lovely thing to seek out and pour over old photographs and videos of our performances (some of which I can't even remember doing), and to show them to my two teenage children, Rua and Ramsay. To hear them repeating some of the Victor and Barry lines and

laughing along with the songs, means so much to me. Alan first got to meet my kids when they were wee. I was in New York with them and my wife Melanie in 2011. I was performing as Jaques in *As You Like It* with the RSC at the Armory. While I was working, Alan kindly took them to the premiere of *The Smurfs* movie. Alan also invited us all for a trip up to his home in the Catskills. I remember Alan playing the Victor and Barry single on his little record player one evening. We all listened as we looked out on to the starlit mountains. Time slightly stopped. It was a magic, memorable moment.

In 2021, Alan came to Stratford Upon Avon and saw me perform as the Police Chief in *The Magician's Elephant* at the RSC. I was so nervous.

In 2022, I saw Alan in Glasgow performing *Burn* and I was so proud to see my old pal up there on the Theatre Royal stage again, strutting his stuff, another hit in the multitude of Alan's wonderful achievements. But then, when I saw that beautiful young boy with the amazing eyes back in 1982, I knew he was something special. I feel utterly blessed to have had the privilege and joy to have spent time with him, onstage and off.

Alan

Inventing the reasons for Victor and Barry's disappearance from showbiz life for the opening chapter, embodying them again as we were improvising and riffing ideas was like stepping back in time. We were helpless with laughter, and I felt such a huge swell of nostalgia for those early years when we were two daft laddies who just clicked and made each other ache with laughter.

Forbes

Working on this book together, has rekindled a fire, not just of our almost-fraternal deep-rooted love, but a desire to do something else together before the curtains close. Oh Dearie Me!

Alan

Yes, we're no awa tae bide awa!

Back in the Day

Do youse remember the 1980s?
They seem a world away
But way back in the 1980s
We were both openly...
Fey...
In the bar at the Tron
We sang song after song
In an amateur way
Back in the day
Back in our hey
Hey hey
Hey
Hey hey
Day
Uh huh

Think back to the 1980s
When the rich still paid their fair share
of tax
We looked arty and so creaty
In our monogrammed blazers and rayon
slacks
And paisley patterned cravats
With our hair gelled flat
We caused laughter attacks
Back in the day
When we were
Barry McLeish and Victor MacIlvaney

When we were Victor and Barry
We were the boys from Kelvinside

But 40 years have passed
And now the days are flying faster
We have plastered over cracks
And here we are back again
It's all watter under the bridges
For these two theatrical weegies
Who are back as BFFs
Yes we're forever friends
to the end

(Dance break)

It's no longer the 1980s
A fact we cannae deny
Just like the fact of you and I
No matter how hard we try
To run and hide
Somewhere down deep inside
Our hearts are tied

Cause we will always be
The boys from Kelvinside